D0893252

Ethics
Desk Reference
for Psychologists

Ethics
Desk Reference
for Psychologists

Jeffrey E. Barnett and W. Brad Johnson

American Psychological Association • Washington, DC

Second Printing May 2010

Published by
American Psychological Association
750 First Street, NE
Washington, DC 20002
www.apa.org

BF76.4
.B37
2008

0183392354

To order
APA Order Department
P.O. Box 92984
Washington, DC 20090-2984
Tel: (800) 374-2721; Direct: (202) 336-5510
Fax: (202) 336-5502; TDD/TTY: (202) 336-6123
Online: www.apa.org/books/
E-mail: order@apa.org

In the U.K., Europe, Africa, and the Middle East, copies may be ordered from
American Psychological Association
3 Henrietta Street
Covent Garden, London
WC2E 8LU England

Typeset in Stone Serif by Circle Graphics, Columbia, MD

Printer: Edwards Brothers, Inc., Ann Arbor, MI
Cover Designer: Mercury Publishing Services, Rockville, MD
Technical/Production Editor: Dan Brachtesende

The opinions and statements published are the responsibility of the authors, and such opinions and statements do not necessarily represent the policies of the American Psychological Association.

Library of Congress Cataloging-in-Publication Data

Barnett, Jeffrey E.
  Ethics desk reference for psychologists / Jeffrey E. Barnett and
W. Brad Johnson.
    p. cm.
  Includes index.
  ISBN-13: 978-1-4338-0352-9
  ISBN-10: 1-4338-0352-6
1. Psychologists—Professional ethics. 2. Psychology—Standards.
I. Johnson, W. Brad. II. Title.

BF76.4.B37 2008
174'.915—dc22
                              2007049383

British Library Cataloguing-in-Publication Data
A CIP record is available from the British Library.

Printed in the United States of America
First Edition

Dedicated to our colleague and friend, Stephen Behnke, JD, PhD, Director of the APA Ethics Office, a great leader who inspires us daily to achieve the highest ethical ideals of our profession.

Contents

PREFACE   *ix*

Part I

The APA Ethics Code

Introduction and Applicability   *3*

Preamble   *9*

General Principles   *11*

    Principle A: Beneficence and Nonmaleficence   *13*

    Principle B: Fidelity and Responsibility   *15*

    Principle C: Integrity   *17*

    Principle D: Justice   *19*

    Principle E: Respect for People's Rights and Dignity   *21*

Ethical Standards   *23*

    Standard 1.   Resolving Ethical Issues   *25*

    Standard 2.   Competence   *41*

    Standard 3.   Human Relations   *57*

    Standard 4.   Privacy and Confidentiality   *79*

    Standard 5.   Advertising and Other Public Statements   *91*

    Standard 6.   Record Keeping and Fees   *101*

    Standard 7.   Education and Training   *113*

Standard 8. Research and Publication *123*

Standard 9. Assessment *145*

Standard 10. Therapy *161*

Part II

Decision Making and Ethical Practice in Specific Areas

Making an Ethical Decision: A Process Model *177*

Managed Care *181*

Clinical Supervision and Consultation *185*

Suicidal Clients *189*

Mandatory Reporting Requirements *193*

Termination and Abandonment *197*

Responding to an Ethics Complaint, Licensure Board Complaint, or Malpractice Suit *201*

APPENDIX: KEY ETHICS RESOURCES FOR PSYCHOLOGISTS *205*

INDEX *209*

ABOUT THE AUTHORS *217*

Preface

The *Ethics Desk Reference for Psychologists* (EDR) is designed to be an accessible, useful, and convenient guide to understanding and applying the American Psychological Association's (APA's) "Ethical Principles of Psychologists and Code of Conduct" (the APA Ethics Code).[1] Each section of the Ethics Code is reprinted here accompanied by a brief review that emphasizes practical application, common dilemmas, and specific strategies for prevention and positive practice. Although understanding the intent and appropriate application of the APA Ethics Code is vitally important for all psychologists, the Code alone cannot provide all the answers for individuals faced with ethical dilemmas. Therefore, guidance on ethical decision making and a step-by-step decision-making model are provided to augment the use of the Ethics Code.

Psychologists work in challenging times. While striving to serve their clients, psychologists must be cognizant of numerous laws, regulations, and ethics standards and be prepared to address novel and complicated dilemmas in their teaching, research, and clinical work. Too often, psychologists may feel threatened by the specter of making an error, missing an important detail, or becoming the focus of a complaint, lawsuit, or other disciplinary action.

---

[1]American Psychological Association. (2010). *Ethical principles of psychologists and code of conduct (2002, Amended June 1, 2010)*. Retrieved from http://www.apa.org/ethics/code/index.aspx

In response, these psychologists may adopt a defensive or risk management approach to their work. From this perspective, the key question is, "How can I protect myself and avoid any possible appearance of imperfection and culpability?" Of course, this strategy can lead to fear-based practice and rarely benefits those with whom psychologists work. In the EDR, we encourage psychologists to be thorough and careful yet positive—versus defensive—in their approach to upholding the highest standards of the Ethics Code. To that end, the EDR includes a section titled "Prevention and Positive Practice" under each standard. The focus here is on doing the right thing, working in advance to provide ethical care, and avoiding a mindset that focuses only on damage control or risk management.

Additionally, the EDR provides up-to-date resources designed to expedite consultation when facing an ethical dilemma. The EDR should serve as a valuable resource for all practicing psychologists, including clinicians, researchers, trainees (interns, postdoctoral fellows, etc.), and their supervisees in all settings, and graduate students as they endeavor to achieve the highest ethical aspirations of the profession. Each psychologist's EDR should be used regularly to guide him or her in achieving ethical excellence.

PART I

THE APA
ETHICS CODE

Prior to World War II the profession of psychology was focused primarily on research and teaching. During the war, psychologists played a significant role in the areas of assessment and treatment. As the profession evolved and psychologists' roles expanded, leaders in the field became convinced that the discipline of psychology would be enhanced and protected through the development of an ethics code. Leaders in the American Psychological Association (APA) appointed a task force to study this issue in 1948. They conducted a critical incident survey of the APA's approximately 2,500 members (there are now approximately 150,000 members!). Each member was asked to describe an ethical dilemma recently faced in his or her work as a psychologist. The responses offered a representative sample of the range of ethics issues and challenges faced by psychologists at that time. These data guided drafting of the initial version of the APA Ethics Code, the "Ethical Standards of Psychologists." It was approved by APA's governing body and implemented in 1953.

Over the years, as the profession of psychology has evolved, so too has the APA Ethics Code. Thus far, it has been revised nine times. The current version was approved in 2002 and implemented in 2003. The Ethics Code is revised and updated to reflect changes in the profession and in the roles in which psychologists serve, developments in the knowledge base in psychology, and changes in societal standards. It is a living document that will continue to be revised and updated periodically to keep it relevant to the times in which psychologists live and work.

Structure and Applicability of the American Psychological Association's Ethics Code

The APA Ethics Code comprises four sections: Introduction and Applicability, Preamble, General Principles, and Ethical Standards. The Introduction and Applicability section describes the intended use and limitations of the Ethics Code and how it may be used in the process of ethical decision making. The Preamble and General Principles highlight the underlying values of the profession, the moral framework on which the Ethics Code is built. One never fully achieves the principles; they are aspirational in nature and are intended to provide guidance for pursuing the highest ideals of the profession in all of psychologists' endeavors. As such, the Preamble and General Principles are not specifically enforceable; however, they provide the foundation for the Ethical Standards that follow. These Ethical Standards are enforceable (by the APA Ethics Committee) and provide the specific standards of professional conduct expected of each member of APA as well as those affiliate state, provincial, and territorial psychological associations that have adopted the standards of the APA Ethics Code. It is also important to note that many states have accepted the APA Ethics Code as legally binding for licensed psychologists practicing in their jurisdiction. Others have used it as the basis for their own ethics codes. Finally, the obligation to abide by the Ethical Standards is often an explicit expectation for students and trainees in graduate programs and training sites.

Introduction and Applicability

The American Psychological Association's (APA's) Ethical Principles of Psychologists and Code of Conduct (hereinafter referred to as the Ethics Code) consists of an Introduction, a Preamble, five General Principles (A–E), and specific Ethical Standards. The Introduction discusses the intent, organization, procedural considerations, and scope of application of the Ethics Code. The Preamble and General Principles are aspirational goals to guide psychologists toward the highest ideals of psychology. Although the Preamble and General Principles are not themselves enforceable rules, they should be considered by psychologists in arriving at an ethical course of action. The Ethical Standards set forth enforceable rules for conduct as psychologists. Most of the Ethical Standards are written broadly, in order to apply to psychologists in varied roles, although the application of an Ethical Standard may vary depending on the context. The Ethical Standards are not exhaustive. The fact that a given conduct is not specifically addressed by an Ethical Standard does not mean that it is necessarily either ethical or unethical.

This Ethics Code applies only to psychologists' activities that are part of their scientific, educational, or professional roles as psychologists. Areas covered include but are not limited to the clinical, counseling, and school practice of psychology; research; teaching; supervision of trainees; public service; policy development; social intervention; development of assessment instruments; conducting assessments; educational counseling; organizational consulting; forensic activities; program design and evaluation; and administration. This Ethics Code applies to these activities across a variety of contexts, such as in person, postal, telephone, Internet, and other electronic transmissions. These activities shall be distinguished from the purely private conduct of psychologists, which is not within the purview of the Ethics Code.

Membership in the APA commits members and student affiliates to comply with the standards of the APA Ethics Code and to the rules and procedures used to enforce them. Lack of awareness or misunderstanding of an Ethical Standard is not itself a defense to a charge of unethical conduct.

The procedures for filing, investigating, and resolving complaints of unethical conduct are described in the current Rules and Procedures of the APA Ethics Committee. APA may impose sanctions on its members for violations of the standards of the Ethics Code, including termination of APA membership, and may notify other bodies and individuals of its actions. Actions that violate the standards of the Ethics Code may also lead to the imposition of sanctions on psychologists or students whether or not they are APA members by bodies other than APA, including state psychological associations, other professional groups, psychology boards, other state or federal agencies, and payors for health services. In addition, APA may take action against a member after his or her conviction of a felony, expulsion or suspension from an affiliated state psychological association, or suspension or loss of licensure. When the sanction to be imposed by APA is less than expulsion, the 2001 Rules and Procedures do not guarantee an opportunity for an in-person hearing, but generally provide that complaints will be resolved only on the basis of a submitted record.

The Ethics Code is intended to provide guidance for psychologists and standards of professional conduct that can be applied by the APA and by other bodies that choose to adopt them. The Ethics Code is not intended to be a basis of civil liability. Whether a psychologist has violated the Ethics Code standards does not by itself determine whether the psychologist is legally liable in a court action, whether a contract is enforceable, or whether other legal consequences occur.

The modifiers used in some of the standards of this Ethics Code (e.g., *reasonably, appropriate, potentially*) are included in the standards when they would (1) allow professional judgment on the part of psychologists, (2) eliminate injustice or inequality that would occur without the modifier, (3) ensure applicability across the broad range of activities conducted by psychologists, or (4) guard against a set of rigid rules that might be quickly outdated. As used in this Ethics Code, the term *reasonable* means the prevailing professional judgment of psychologists engaged in similar activities in similar circumstances, given the knowledge the psychologist had or should have had at the time.

In the process of making decisions regarding their professional behavior, psychologists must consider this Ethics Code in addition to applicable laws and psychology board regulations. In applying the Ethics Code to their professional work, psychologists may consider other materials and guidelines that have been adopted or endorsed by scientific and professional psychological organizations and the dictates of their own conscience, as well as consult with others within the field. If this Ethics Code establishes a higher standard of conduct than is required by law, psychologists must meet the higher ethical standard. If psychologists' ethical responsibilities conflict with law, regulations, or other governing legal authority, psychologists make known their commitment to this Ethics Code and take steps to resolve the conflict in a responsible manner in keeping with basic principles of human rights.

Essential Elements

- The Ethical Standards are broadly written to cover the wide range of professional activities engaged in by psychologists to include all functions, roles, work settings, populations served, and media used.
- The Ethical Standards are not intended to address every dilemma psychologists could possibly face; in situations not specifically addressed in the standards, psychologists are to use the General Principles for guidance in their decision making.
- The Ethical Standards must be read and applied in specific contexts; interpretation of standards must be guided by unique circumstances and specific modifiers in the standards themselves (e.g., *reasonably, appropriate, potentially*).
- The standards of the Ethics Code are directly relevant to all aspects of each psychologist's functioning as a psychologist. In addition, in those areas in which a psychologist's personal life impacts his or her professional activities (e.g., substance abuse impacting a psychologist's clinical competence with clients) the Ethics Code will be relevant for guiding a psychologist's decisions and behavior. The purely private conduct of a psychologist is not subject to the Ethics Code.
- All fellows, members, and student affiliates of the APA are held to the standards of the APA Ethics Code.
- Lack of knowledge of the Ethics Code or misunderstanding about how to effectively apply it are not themselves considered appropriate justifications for failure to fully follow the Ethics Code.
- The APA may take a range of actions against members who are found in violation of the standards of the Ethics Code. Additionally, the APA may share information about violations with regulatory agencies and other bodies that may take action as well. Further, the APA may take action against members who are convicted of a felony, are expelled or suspended from affiliated state psychological associations, or lose their license to practice.
- The APA Ethics Code is not a legal document, and violation of the Code should not be used as the basis for any civil liability or a basis for legal action. The standards of the

Ethics Code are only applicable to APA members and affiliates and other organizations that choose to adopt it.

- The Ethics Code is worded carefully and uses modifiers such as *reasonably, appropriately,* and *potentially* to ensure that it is not rigidly or inappropriately applied, that it will be relevant to the wide range of activities in which psychologists engage, and to allow for the use of professional judgment of psychologists when applying the Ethics Code.

- The word *reasonable,* as used in the Ethics Code, is defined as "the prevailing professional judgment of psychologists engaged in similar activities in similar circumstances, given the knowledge the psychologist had or should have had at the time." This definition highlights the need to apply the Ethics Code contextually.

- The Ethics Code is a key resource for confronting ethical dilemmas, but the Code alone cannot clearly resolve every ethical dilemma. Psychologists must also rely on relevant laws and regulations, practice guidelines (see the APA Practice Guidelines: http://www.apa.org/practice/prof.html), and the dictates of their conscience.

- When faced with an ethical dilemma, psychologists should routinely consult with knowledgeable colleagues and other resources such as local or national ethics committees.

- When the Ethics Code sets a higher standard than laws and regulations psychologists must follow the dictates of the Ethics Code.

- When the Ethics Code is in conflict with laws or regulations, psychologists must make known their commitment to the Ethics Code and work to resolve the conflict while fulfilling the obligations of the Ethics Code. Psychologists may never use a legal mandate (e.g., law, regulation, statute) as a justification for or defense against violating human rights.

Preamble

Psychologists are committed to increasing scientific and professional knowledge of behavior and people's understanding of themselves and others and to the use of such knowledge to improve the condition of individuals, organizations, and society. Psychologists respect and protect civil and human rights and the central importance of freedom of inquiry and expression in research, teaching, and publication. They strive to help the public in developing informed judgments and choices concerning human behavior. In doing so, they perform many roles, such as researcher, educator, diagnostician, therapist, supervisor, consultant, administrator, social interventionist, and expert witness. This Ethics Code provides a common set of principles and standards upon which psychologists build their professional and scientific work.

This Ethics Code is intended to provide specific standards to cover most situations encountered by psychologists. It has as its goals the welfare and protection of the individuals and groups with whom psychologists work and the education of members, students, and the public regarding ethical standards of the discipline.

The development of a dynamic set of ethical standards for psychologists' work-related conduct requires a personal commitment and lifelong effort to act ethically; to encourage ethical behavior by students, supervisees,

employees, and colleagues; and to consult with others concerning ethical problems.

Essential Elements

- The preamble provides orienting statements about the applicability of the Ethics Code but does not contain enforceable standards.
- Psychologists respect and protect the rights of all those with whom they interact professionally and promote freedom of inquiry and expression in research, teaching, and publication.
- Psychologists promote the autonomous decision making and functioning of others and share sufficient information with others so they can make informed decisions.
- Psychologists carry out the goals and ideals of the Ethics Code in the many diverse professional roles in which they serve.
- The Ethics Code provides the foundation for all professional decisions made by psychologists; the Ethics Code's principles and standards should guide professional activities and decision making.
- Because the Ethics Code can never directly address every dilemma and situation a psychologist could possibly face, psychologists are guided by the goal of promoting the welfare and protection of those they serve.
- Psychologists educate others about the Ethics Code and promote ethical conduct and practice by others in the profession, including those in training.
- All psychologists commit themselves to a career-long effort to fulfill the highest ideals of the APA Ethics Code and to actively promote this commitment in others.
- In their efforts to achieve the highest ethical ideals of their profession, psychologists consult colleagues when faced with ethical dilemmas.

General Principles

This section consists of General Principles. General Principles, as opposed to Ethical Standards, are aspirational in nature. Their intent is to guide and inspire psychologists toward the very highest ethical ideals of the profession. General Principles, in contrast to Ethical Standards, do not represent obligations and should not form the basis for imposing sanctions. Relying upon General Principles for either of these reasons distorts both their meaning and purpose.

Essential Elements

Ethical principles are the core ethical norms for the community of psychologists. Ethical principles are broader and more basic than any specific standard. Unlike the specific standards, which form the bulk of the Ethics Code, principles serve as more general guideposts to the highest ethical ideals of the profession. They are not intended to be enforceable rules. Because the ethical standards cannot address every possible ethical quandary, ethical principles provide foundational values for the profession. These essential ethical goals provide a framework from which to reason ethically.

Prevention and Positive Practice

✓ Consider the General Principles in all ethics decision making.

✓ Recognize that achieving the full intent of the Ethics Code involves aspiring to the highest ethical principles, not just meeting the minimal ethical standards.
✓ Understand the APA principles and standards as working in concert to guide psychologists to behave ethically.
✓ Accept that novel areas of practice, idiosyncratic circumstances, and apparent incongruity between the standards and competing laws and regulations make familiarity with the foundational principles essential.

Principle A: Beneficence and Nonmaleficence

Psychologists strive to benefit those with whom they work and take care to do no harm. In their professional actions, psychologists seek to safeguard the welfare and rights of those with whom they interact professionally and other affected persons, and the welfare of animal subjects of research. When conflicts occur among psychologists' obligations or concerns, they attempt to resolve these conflicts in a responsible fashion that avoids or minimizes harm. Because psychologists' scientific and professional judgments and actions may affect the lives of others, they are alert to and guard against personal, financial, social, organizational, or political factors that might lead to misuse of their influence. Psychologists strive to be aware of the possible effect of their own physical and mental health on their ability to help those with whom they work.

Essential Elements

Psychologists have no more pressing obligations than the complementary moral requirements to help those they serve and to avoid causing harm to anyone affected by their work. The requirement to avoid causing harm includes both intentional harm and harm caused by negligence. When harm is unavoidable, this principle enjoins psychologists to minimize harm as much as possible.

Avoiding harm to persons or animal research subjects is considered a minimal expectation for psychologists. If it is not possible to prevent harm to others entirely, then psychologists must demonstrate that they have made all possible efforts to minimize harm. In addition to avoiding harm, they should always approach professional and ethical decision making with a focus on how to most clearly further their clients' best interests. Their decisions must be driven by the potential for benefit to others. Finally, psychologists must be vigilant to potential misuses of their work and the potential impact of their own health and functioning on their ability to help, and not harm, those with whom they work.

Prevention and Positive Practice

✓ Before determining a course of professional action, weigh potential benefits and risks of harm.

✓ Ask yourself: "Would a jury of my peers agree that I carefully considered risks and benefits and acted to maximize benefit and minimize harm?"

✓ Try to anticipate how other persons, professionals, or organizations might misuse your work and make every effort to prevent such misuse.

✓ Take steps to ensure that your own psychological and physical health does not interfere with your capacity to effectively help those with whom you work.

✓ When conflicts occur with clients, organizations, or between different components of the Ethics Code, take steps to resolve the conflict while minimizing harm and promoting the best interests of your clients.

Principle B: Fidelity and Responsibility

Psychologists establish relationships of trust with those with whom they work. They are aware of their professional and scientific responsibilities to society and to the specific communities in which they work. Psychologists uphold professional standards of conduct, clarify their professional roles and obligations, accept appropriate responsibility for their behavior, and seek to manage conflicts of interest that could lead to exploitation or harm. Psychologists consult with, refer to, or cooperate with other professionals and institutions to the extent needed to serve the best interests of those with whom they work. They are concerned about the ethical compliance of their colleagues' scientific and professional conduct. Psychologists strive to contribute a portion of their professional time for little or no compensation or personal advantage.

Essential Elements

Psychologists are faithful and loyal to their clients, to their colleagues, and to the larger profession of psychology. Because fidelity is central to professional relationships, psychologists carefully nurture trust through truth-telling, promise-keeping, unconditional loyalty, and thorough reliability. In their professional work, psychologists are sensitive to their clients' vulnerability and conscientious regarding the power they hold relative to clients. They demonstrate faithful commitment by working to further the best interests of others and always responding to questions or conflicts with sincere and candid truthfulness. Psychologists also accept full responsibility for their actions and refuse to blame others or avoid accountability for their professional work. Finally, this ethical principle implies loyalty and faithfulness to both colleagues and the broader profession. Each psychologist must be observant of the conduct of colleagues and willing to intervene when concerns arise. Likewise, each psychologist must honor his or her obligation to the profession, recognizing that few things diminish the public trust in psychology more quickly than irresponsible or dishonest behavior.

Prevention and Positive Practice

✓ Be honest with clients, colleagues, and the public.
✓ Be faithful and loyal to those you serve, even when this commitment is inconvenient or difficult.
✓ Accept accountability for all of your professional work; seek to resolve errors in a way that promotes the best interests of those you serve.
✓ Utilize all available resources in your efforts to serve others' best interests.
✓ Confront apparent unethical behavior as a way of being faithful to both your colleagues and the profession.
✓ Offer some of your professional service pro bono as a means of fulfilling the profession's highest ideals of service to those in need.

Principle C: Integrity

Psychologists seek to promote accuracy, honesty, and truthfulness in the science, teaching, and practice of psychology. In these activities psychologists do not steal, cheat, or engage in fraud, subterfuge, or intentional misrepresentation of fact. Psychologists strive to keep their promises and to avoid unwise or unclear commitments. In situations in which deception may be ethically justifiable to maximize benefits and minimize harm, psychologists have a serious obligation to consider the need for, the possible consequences of, and their responsibility to correct any resulting mistrust or other harmful effects that arise from the use of such techniques.

Essential Elements

A psychologist should be upright in all areas of his or her professional life. When a psychologist is dishonest, exploitive, or engages in fraud, he or she stands to do profound harm to individual clients and to the public's perception of psychologists. Each psychologist is obligated to adhere to stringent standards of honesty, truthfulness, accuracy in all of his or her statements, and integrity broadly defined. Because of these requirements, psychologists should be cautious and thoughtful about entering into professional commitments and making promises about what they can deliver. Finally, in the rare circumstances in which deception is justified in clinical, research, or teaching duties, psychologists should be proactive in ensuring that harm is minimized and remediated whenever possible.

Prevention and Positive Practice

- ✓ Be accurate, honest, and transparent in all of your professional work.
- ✓ Make only those promises and commitments you know you can keep.
- ✓ Never take unfair advantage of or mislead those with whom you work.
- ✓ Avoid deception; when deception is clearly justified, work to minimize any harm to the client or subject and damage to the profession.

Principle D: Justice

Psychologists recognize that fairness and justice entitle all persons to access to and benefit from the contributions of psychology and to equal quality in the processes, procedures, and services being conducted by psychologists. Psychologists exercise reasonable judgment and take precautions to ensure that their potential biases, the boundaries of their competence, and the limitations of their expertise do not lead to or condone unjust practices.

Essential Elements

Psychologists must be fair in all of their professional activities. They are obligated to act fairly, to treat others equitably, and to avoid bias and discrimination in their practices. Psychologists must be particularly attentive to ensure equal treatment to all those they serve, regardless of variables such as age, gender, race, ethnicity, religion, sexual orientation, disability, socioeconomic status, and language. Psychologists also have a duty to work against injustice and unfair practices both within the profession of psychology and in society at large.

Prevention and Positive Practice

✓ Treat all those you work with professionally, as you would want to be treated.

✓ Ensure that everyone you work with receives the same high-quality service.
✓ Make your services accessible to the widest range of persons, and refuse to allow demographic or cultural variables to impact accessibility or quality.
✓ Draw attention to and work against unfair or discriminatory practices in your agency, organization, and community.

Principle E: Respect for People's Rights and Dignity

Psychologists respect the dignity and worth of all people, and the rights of individuals to privacy, confidentiality, and self-determination. Psychologists are aware that special safeguards may be necessary to protect the rights and welfare of persons or communities whose vulnerabilities impair autonomous decision making. Psychologists are aware of and respect cultural, individual, and role differences, including those based on age, gender, gender identity, race, ethnicity, culture, national origin, religion, sexual orientation, disability, language, and socioeconomic status and consider these factors when working with members of such groups. Psychologists try to eliminate the effect on their work of biases based on those factors, and they do not knowingly participate in or condone activities of others based upon such prejudices.

Essential Elements

Psychologists respect the inherent dignity and the right to self-determination of all persons. Whenever possible, psychologists work to support those with whom they work in making fully autonomous and independent decisions. Psychologists must respect the fact that their clients, students, and research subjects have the right to rule themselves and live their own lives without interference, even when psychologists do not agree with their decisions. Psychologists must see all those with whom they work as worthy of respect and autonomy and take action to reduce any infringement on clients' freedom and dignity arising from their own biases. This means that each psychologist is obligated to be self-aware and work against biases related to cultural differences or demographic factors. When, because of personal limitations or inadequate understanding, persons cannot make meaningful choices, psychologists work with those persons, their legal guardians, and relevant systems to maximize their autonomy and respect their dignity.

Prevention and Positive Practice

✓ Recognize the inherent dignity and worth of every human being you encounter.

✓ Protect the right to self-determination and free choice in all those you serve.

✓ Safeguard privacy and ensure thorough informed consent as specific ways to respect dignity and facilitate autonomous decision making.

✓ Be familiar with the Guidelines for Providers of Psychological Services to Ethnic, Linguistic, and Culturally Diverse Populations (http://www.apa.org/pi/oema/guide.html); the Guidelines on Multicultural Education, Training, Research, Practice, and Organizational Change for Psychologists (http://www.apa.org/pi/multiculturalguidelines/homepage .html); and the Guidelines for Psychotherapy With Lesbian, Gay, and Bisexual Clients (http://www.apadivision44.org/ resources/apa_guidelines.php) as a way of reducing biases that may interfere with your capacity to accord dignity and support autonomy in those with whom you work.

✓ Seek consultation when you find it difficult to allow clients, students, or research subjects to be fully independent in their actions and decisions.

✓ Develop and maintain knowledge and competence in the assessment and treatment of diverse individuals as defined in this principle.

Ethical Standards

In contrast to the Ethical Principles, which are purely aspirational in nature, the Ethical Standards of the American Psychological Association (APA) Ethics Code set forth enforceable rules for conduct as psychologists. The Ethical Standards are written broadly so that they will fit psychologists' varied roles. In addition, the standards frequently contain qualifying language (e.g., "whenever feasible") to allow psychologists some measure of flexibility in determining how to apply the standard in a specific professional context. Although the precise application of an Ethical Standard may vary depending on the unique circumstances faced by a psychologist, all of the Ethical Standards are enforceable. Each standard is written with enough specificity that psychology boards and associations that adopt the APA Ethics Code may clearly enforce the standard. Consider the Ethical Standards to be *rules of the road* for ethical practice as a psychologist. Psychologists may be sanctioned for violating any Ethical Standard. Finally, just because a given behavior or practice is not specifically mentioned by an Ethical Standard does not mean that it is either ethical or unethical. In these cases, good judgment and collegial consultation are paramount.

In the following sections of the *Ethics Desk Reference for Psychologists*, each Ethical Standard is briefly distilled to its essential elements, and common dilemmas and problems related to each standard are described. Each section ends with a clear list of recommendations for engaging in proactive, preventative, and positive practice as a psychologist. These recommendations are designed to help psychologists achieve professional excellence, not merely compliance with each standard.

Standard 1. Resolving Ethical Issues

1.01 Misuse of Psychologists' Work

If psychologists learn of misuse or misrepresentation of their work, they take reasonable steps to correct or minimize the misuse or misrepresentation.

Essential Elements

At some point, a psychologist's professional work may be misused. Quite often, a psychologist will be unaware of misuse or misrepresentation of his or her work until a colleague brings it to the psychologist's attention or he or she happens on the misuse by chance—perhaps while reading a newspaper or journal article. At times, a psychologist's research findings, public comments, or even clinical work may be taken out of context and misapplied to support a political agenda. Even though the psychologist may not be responsible for the misuse of the work, he or she does have an obligation to take reasonable steps to rectify the situation once aware of it. Thus, if a news story misrepresents a psychologist's work, a letter to the editor requesting a correction or retraction would be quite appropriate. Failure to respond to evidence of misuse conveys tacit approval and would be unethical.

Common Dilemmas and Conflicts

- It is unreasonable to expect psychologists to be aware of every misuse of their work, but it is reasonable to expect them to take action once misuse becomes evident or is brought to their attention.

■ Research findings, assessment results, clinical techniques, and even comments in professional presentations are all vulnerable to misuse and misrepresentation.

■ At times, psychologists who become aware that their work has been misused may respond with dysfunctional anger and accusation, further exacerbating the situation.

■ Even when an author or clinician is well acquainted with the American Psychological Association (APA) Ethics Code and appropriate in qualifying his or her work, those who interpret, apply, and cite the psychologist's work may not show due regard for ethical standards.

■ At times, even the most cordial efforts to address misuse of one's work are unsuccessful; the psychologist must then decide whether to take formal action to correct the problem or protect the public.

Prevention and Positive Practice

✓ First, prevent misuse of your work by clarifying the limitations of all data, appropriate interpretations of findings, and valid applications of techniques up front. Also, clearly reference any sections of the APA Ethics Code relevant to how your work should be used.

✓ Be vigilant to references to your work in both professional and popular forums to increase the probability of early detection of misuse.

✓ When you learn that your work may have been misused or misrepresented, take immediate steps to investigate and verify the problem. Cordially but clearly confront and educate the individual or organization about the misuse of your work and its implications. Make a specific request for corrective action within a clear time frame.

✓ If attempts to resolve the issue informally are ineffective, consider a more formal action such as filing an ethics complaint.

✓ Carefully document the sequence of events and your efforts to correct or minimize the misuse, and consult with colleagues and resources such as ethics committees and the APA Ethics Office.

1.02 Conflicts Between Ethics and Law, Regulations, or Other Governing Legal Authority[1]

If psychologists' ethical responsibilities conflict with law, regulations, or other governing legal authority, psychologists clarify the nature of the conflict, make known their commitment to the Ethics Code, and take reasonable steps to resolve the conflict consistent with the General Principles and Ethical Standards of the Ethics Code. Under no circumstances may this standard be used to justify or defend violating human rights.

Essential Elements

Although psychologists are clearly bound to honor the principles and standards of the APA Ethics Code, they must simultaneously remain cognizant of relevant laws and regulations bearing on their work. An ethical psychologist remains alert to real or potential conflicts between ethical and legal requirements in his or her professional setting. When conflicts emerge, psychologists must be proactive in attempting to resolve them, and in so doing, must affirm an abiding commitment to the Ethics Code. If, in spite of a psychologist's best efforts, a workable solution is not achieved, the Ethics Code allows psychologists to adhere to laws and regulations unless doing so would violate human rights. It is essential to remember that the Ethics Code does not *require* adherence to laws and regulations: At times, perhaps as a matter of conscience, a psychologist may defy a legal requirement in order to uphold a salient ethical principle or standard. Psychologists never have the option of adhering to a legal requirement when doing so would violate another person's human rights.

Common Dilemmas and Conflicts

- Psychologists who are unaware of the regulatory environment in which they function may overlook relevant

---

[1]Standard 1.02 is newly worded, following amendments passed by the APA Council of Representatives, effective June 1, 2010. For background on this change, see American Psychological Association. (in press). Report of the Ethics Committee, 2009. *American Psychologist.* doi:10.1037/a0019515

regulations or laws that directly impact their professional roles.

- Ignorance regarding possible conflicts between ethics and laws, regulations, and other legal requirements is not an adequate defense should adverse consequences occur for clients.
- Psychologists may occasionally feel "stuck" between ethical obligations and local or federal legal requirements and may indeed be forced to choose between the two.
- Psychologists functioning in highly regulated environments such as forensic settings, law enforcement, the military, and the Veterans Administration are likely to experience more frequent conflicts between ethics and laws or regulations.
- Psychologists may erroneously assume that they *must* comply with legal mandates even when these statutes jeopardize human rights.

Prevention and Positive Practice

✓ Educate yourself regarding all laws and regulations relevant to your practice setting.

✓ Anticipate potential conflicts and make ongoing efforts at prevention through open discussions with clients and stakeholders.

✓ Educate those in positions of authority regarding the APA Ethics Code and your obligations under it.

✓ Engage in active consultation with experienced colleagues, ethics committees, the APA Ethics Office, or legal counsel when confronted by ethical–legal conflicts. This is especially important when questions about human rights arise.

✓ Always make an effort to resolve ethical–legal conflicts flexibly, creatively, and with your clients' best interests at heart.

✓ When an ethical–legal conflict remains intractable despite your best efforts at prevention and resolution, go on the record regarding your commitment to the APA Ethics Code and then seek consultation before deciding whether to abide by the law or regulation.

✓ Before deciding on a course of civil disobedience—a valid moral and ethical stance in some cases and a requirement if a law violates human rights—seek legal and ethical consultation as well as support from professional organizations.

1.03 Conflicts Between Ethics and Organizational Demands[2]

If the demands of an organization with which psychologists are affiliated or for whom they are working are in conflict with this Ethics Code, psychologists clarify the nature of the conflict, make known their commitment to the Ethics Code, and take reasonable steps to resolve the conflict consistent with the General Principles and Ethical Standards of the Ethics Code. Under no circumstances may this standard be used to justify or defend violating human rights.

Essential Elements

Just as a psychologist's obligations under the Ethics Code may conflict with laws and regulations (Standard 1.02), ethical obligations occasionally conflict with organizational demands. Psychologists who are employed by or consult with any organization may find themselves caught between ethical and organizational demands. However, unlike legal requirements, organizational demands may never trump a psychologist's obligation to the Ethics Code. Regardless of the outcome of efforts to resolve ethical–organizational conflicts, careful adherence to the Ethics Code is expected. Psychologists must never support or comply with organizational demands that violate human rights.

Common Dilemmas and Conflicts

- Psychologists offering services within or in consultation with organizations are at risk when they fail to anticipate competing demands and conflicts of interest between the concerns of individuals and organizations.
- Organizational demands do not offer suitable justification for overlooking or violating any portion of the Ethics Code, or human rights.

---

[2]Standard 1.03 is newly worded, following amendments passed by the APA Council of Representatives, effective June 1, 2010. For background on this change, see American Psychological Association. (in press). Report of the Ethics Committee, 2009. *American Psychologist.* doi:10.1037/a0019515

- Psychologists who fail to demonstrate a good faith effort to anticipate, prevent, and expeditiously resolve ethical–organizational conflicts are at risk in this area.

Prevention and Positive Practice

✓ If you plan to consult with organizations, seek appropriate education and supervision in this area of practice.

✓ Educate key stakeholders in your organization regarding the Ethics Code and your obligations under it; this includes your fundamental obligation to safeguard human rights.

✓ During the formative stage of accepting a job or establishing a consulting relationship with an organization, anticipate likely ethical–organizational conflicts and demonstrate a thorough effort at prevention.

✓ Be alert to common ethical–organizational conflicts (e.g., multiple relationships; identification of the primary client; administration, storage, and control of assessment information; confidentiality; unintended use of your work), and discuss these in advance with clients and stakeholders as a means of providing informed consent.

✓ Engage in consultation with experienced colleagues when conflicts arise.

✓ Attempt to resolve ethical–organizational conflicts with the interests of both individual and organizational clients in mind and with your obligations to the Ethics Code as your primary guide.

1.04 Informal Resolution of Ethical Violations

When psychologists believe that there may have been an ethical violation by another psychologist, they attempt to resolve the issue by bringing it to the attention of that individual, if an informal resolution appears appropriate and the intervention does not violate any confidentiality rights that may be involved. (See also Standards 1.02, Conflicts Between Ethics and Law, Regulations, or Other Governing Legal Authority, and 1.03, Conflicts Between Ethics and Organizational Demands.)

Essential Elements

Sooner or later, all psychologists will encounter an apparent breach of the Ethics Code on the part of a colleague. Every psychologist is ethically obligated to address unethical behavior on the part of other psychologists. This peer intervention requirement is vital to protecting clients, the public at large, and the profession of psychology. Whenever possible, psychologists should attempt to resolve the problem informally by bringing the concern or evidence to the attention of the psychologist, explaining the relevant ethical issues, and seeking an adequate solution. Such respectful and forthright informal interventions are not only likely to elicit cooperation but they may also reveal evidence of misunderstanding regarding the ethical concern. If an informal resolution does not succeed or if the nature of the unethical behavior is so severe that it is perhaps likely to cause significant harm, then a formal ethics complaint may be indicated. Whenever an informal or formal collegial intervention is made, psychologists should be careful to protect the confidentiality and privacy of any client(s) involved.

Common Dilemmas and Conflicts

- It is never pleasant to confront a colleague; however, psychologists must take responsibility for protecting the public and protecting the image of psychology.
- Psychologists who frame informal peer confrontation as a personal attack, versus an opportunity to save a colleague and clients from bad outcomes, are less inclined to respond effectively.
- It is unethical to ignore evidence of peer misconduct.
- As a result of power differentials in psychologists' work settings or fear of repercussions, it may be tempting to rationalize that someone else should confront the colleague or to hope that the situation will resolve on its own.
- Psychologists who are quick to assume that a colleague has been unethical or who adopt an aggressive and accusing approach are likely to be ineffective.
- Even when a colleague's behavior is clearly unethical, a psychologist's desire to take action must not supersede respect for clients' privacy rights.

Prevention and Positive Practice

✓ First, consider whether a client's privacy and confidentiality rights limit your ability to speak directly with your colleague.

✓ Speak respectfully with your colleague if you have concern regarding possible unethical behavior. Be collegial and refrain from making unfounded accusations.

✓ Clearly explain your concerns and point out the relevant sections of the APA Ethics Code.

✓ Use good judgment in deciding whether the matter is appropriate for informal resolution; informal resolution is generally appropriate for minor violations of the APA Ethics Code and violations that are not likely to cause substantial harm to clients.

✓ When attempts at informal resolution are unsuccessful or if it appears that simple educational efforts will not be sufficient, document your attempt at informal resolution and consider filing a formal complaint with an appropriate licensing board or ethics committee. Such reports should only occur with the appropriate written consent of those whose privacy you are obligated to protect.

✓ When the colleague in question is a supervisor, faculty member, employer, or a person with whom you have an ongoing relationship, it is important to seek consultation with a respected colleague or mentor before determining the best course of action.

✓ Reframe informal resolution efforts as an opportunity to prevent a colleague from making a more egregious error and an opportunity to protect the public's perception of psychology.

✓ If you are informally counseled by a peer concerning ethical problems, consider yourself fortunate, avoid defensiveness, take measures to correct any unethical behavior immediately, and sincerely thank your colleague.

1.05 Reporting Ethical Violations

If an apparent ethical violation has substantially harmed or is likely to substantially harm a person or organization and is not appropriate for informal resolution under Standard 1.04, Informal Resolution of Ethical Violations,

or is not resolved properly in that fashion, psychologists take further action appropriate to the situation. Such action might include referral to state or national committees on professional ethics, to state licensing boards, or to the appropriate institutional authorities. This standard does not apply when an intervention would violate confidentiality rights or when psychologists have been retained to review the work of another psychologist whose professional conduct is in question. (See also Standard 1.02, Conflicts Between Ethics and Law, Regulations, or Other Governing Legal Authority.)

Essential Elements

When efforts at informal resolution of apparent unethical behavior by a colleague are either ineffective or inappropriate, psychologists have an ethical obligation to file a formal complaint. As is relevant and appropriate, a psychologist may file a complaint with the APA Ethics Committee, a state, provincial, or territorial psychological association (SPTPA) ethics committee, a psychology licensure board, or other relevant regulatory agencies such as institutional review boards or other oversight agencies. If the other psychologist is not a member of APA or an SPTPA, then filing a complaint with a state licensure board is typically appropriate. When unsure whether an informal resolution of an ethics complaint is the most appropriate course, consult with colleagues and with these agencies themselves. When determining whether it is appropriate to file an ethics complaint, the standard to apply is the presence or likelihood of substantial harm to clients or organizations. A formal complaint may also be indicated if a psychologist has a legitimate concern about direct confrontation of another psychologist such as fear of retaliation or clear power differential. As always, it is never appropriate to violate a client's confidentiality to file an ethics complaint. Psychologists are not bound by this standard when serving on an ethics committee or other regulatory board or when retained to review the work of another psychologist whose professional conduct is in question.

Common Dilemmas and Conflicts

- Filing a complaint against another psychologist may cause feelings of anxiety or guilt.

- Deciding where to file a complaint may seem challenging, especially when a colleague falls under the jurisdiction of multiple disciplinary bodies.
- When a psychologist becomes aware of harmful, exploitative, or otherwise unethical behavior that appears to have caused or is likely to cause substantial harm, it is possible to compound harm by taking action without the written consent of the affected individual(s).
- Filing a formal ethics complaint prematurely, that is, before obtaining reasonable evidence that substantial harm has occurred or is likely, is a misuse of the ethics complaint process. In these situations informal resolution should first be attempted.
- Irrefutable proof of an egregious ethics violation is rare. Using this unrealistic standard as a threshold for filing a complaint may result in further harm to the public and the profession.

Prevention and Positive Practice

✓ When deciding whether or where to file a formal ethics complaint, consult with an experienced colleague or the APA Ethics Office for advice.

✓ During consultation, take time to honestly explore any personal motivations for either filing (e.g., revenge) or not filing (e.g., friendship, discomfort) an ethics complaint.

✓ Do not file simultaneous complaints through multiple organizations. Select the one you feel is most appropriate on the basis of the individual's organizational memberships and licensure status. Accessing organizational membership directories or licensure rosters may be helpful. The APA Membership Directory is available online at http://www.apa.org/databases/mem_directory/.

✓ Before filing a complaint, gather as much information as possible about the alleged infraction(s) and the individuals involved. This information will be invaluable to ethics committees in appraising the evidence and conducting a formal investigation.

✓ When confidentiality issues are involved, obtain the written consent of all affected parties before filing a complaint.

You do not want to compound the situation by violating privacy rights.

✓ When a psychologist is already under investigation and you are consulted by the investigating agency as an ethics expert, there is no need to file an additional complaint as a result of your consultation work.

1.06 Cooperating With Ethics Committees

Psychologists cooperate in ethics investigations, proceedings, and resulting requirements of the APA or any affiliated state psychological association to which they belong. In doing so, they address any confidentiality issues. Failure to cooperate is itself an ethics violation. However, making a request for deferment of adjudication of an ethics complaint pending the outcome of litigation does not alone constitute noncooperation.

Essential Elements

If a formal complaint is filed against a psychologist, regardless of its credibility or veracity, the psychologist must cooperate fully with any resulting investigation. Although this requirement applies to the APA Ethics Committee, it may also apply to other organizations such as SPTPAs and licensing boards, if they have adopted the APA Ethics Code. Psychologists are also obligated to cooperate fully with any hearing or proceeding resulting from the complaint. Further, if an ethics committee finds a psychologist in violation of the Ethics Code and stipulates additional education, training, supervision, or other remediation, the psychologist must comply. Failure to cooperate fully with an ethics committee is itself an ethics violation. If a malpractice suit or other litigation is also pending, it is appropriate to request a deferral of any ethics committee investigation pending the outcome of the legal matter.

Common Dilemmas and Conflicts

■ Although psychologists are busy professionals, failure to respond to an ethics complaint in a timely manner will likely only compound matters and may result in additional charges and consequences.

- Even if an ethics complaint appears to be unsubstantiated or frivolous, full cooperation with the ethics committee is the only acceptable response.
- Emotions such as shock, anxiety, anger, and shame—although common on learning one is the focus of a complaint—can provoke self-sabotaging impulsivity, defensiveness, or withholding when responding to the complaint.
- Psychologists who know the identity of the complainant may be tempted to try and resolve the matter informally. Such efforts may backfire, and they never absolve the psychologist of the obligation to cooperate fully with the ethics committee.
- Although an ethics committee may grant a psychologist's request to defer an investigation pending the outcome of a related lawsuit, assuming that the deferral is automatic is unwise.
- Assuming—without verifying—that all confidentiality issues have been addressed when responding to an ethics complaint may further compound a psychologist's difficulties.

Prevention and Positive Practice

✓ Avoid responding impulsively to an ethics complaint; seek consultation, collegial support, and legal counsel as you prepare a thorough, thoughtful, and timely response.

✓ Consider full cooperation with an ethics investigation, proceeding, or resulting requirement a mandate. Failure to cooperate fully and in a timely manner will likely be viewed as a violation of the APA Ethics Code.

✓ When unsure of your specific obligations to a committee, ask! Always communicate in writing and send letters by certified mail to ensure they have been received; create a paper trail of your reasonable good faith efforts to cooperate.

✓ All requests for a deferral of an investigation should be made in writing.

✓ Always require written consent from affected parties before sharing their confidential information, even with an ethics investigator.

✓ With appropriate consent, share all information and materials relevant to the matter being investigated.

✓ Familiarize yourself with the "Rules and Procedures" of the APA Ethics Office to know your rights, obligations, and responsibilities in responding to a complaint (available at http://www.apa.org/ethics/rules.html).

✓ When specific requirements for education, remediation, or other actions result from the outcome of an ethics proceeding, be sure you fully understand what is being required of you and be sure to comply fully within mandated time limits.

1.07 Improper Complaints

Psychologists do not file or encourage the filing of ethics complaints that are made with reckless disregard for or willful ignorance of facts that would disprove the allegation.

Essential Elements

Ethics complaints should only be filed when a legitimate concern exists and when evidence truly indicates that a violation of the APA Ethics Code may have occurred. The ethics complaint process should not be used as a weapon against those with whom psychologists are aggrieved. Psychologists should endeavor to prevent their personal biases, prejudices, conflicts, or views of others from influencing decisions about ethics complaints. They must also refrain from encouraging others to misuse the ethics complaint process.

Common Dilemmas and Conflicts

- Although at times psychologists may be offended, angered, frustrated, or put off by other professionals, using the APA Ethics Code as a weapon for personal reasons is never considered appropriate.
- Using the threat of a complaint to abuse the trust others put in psychologists or to abuse the power differential in professional relationships is unethical.
- Exaggerating facts or omitting important facts that would disprove allegations to justify filing a complaint against a colleague violates the Ethics Code.

- Encouraging others to engage in any of these actions—particularly those one supervises or employs—is equally abusive and inappropriate.
- Psychologists who file a countercomplaint against a complainant with the intent of punishing or harassing that person are behaving unethically.

Prevention and Positive Practice

✓ When conflicts with colleagues arise, attempt to resolve them professionally and with tact. Never use the APA Ethics Code and the filing of an ethics complaint as a means of pursuing vendettas or settling disagreements that do not involve clearly unethical behaviors.

✓ Never use the filing of an ethics complaint as a punitive measure. Take this step only in compliance with Standards 1.04 and 1.05.

✓ Keep in mind that all complaints will trigger a careful investigation. All relevant facts will be revealed, including the role of the complainant. Be sure you have adequate information and genuine interest in protecting the public before filing a complaint.

1.08 Unfair Discrimination Against Complainants and Respondents

Psychologists do not deny persons employment, advancement, admissions to academic or other programs, tenure, or promotion, based solely upon their having made or their being the subject of an ethics complaint. This does not preclude taking action based upon the outcome of such proceedings or considering other appropriate information.

Essential Elements

When a psychologist becomes the focus of an ethics complaint or has filed a complaint, he or she should be accorded due process and respectful treatment from both colleagues and ethics committees. It is a violation of the Ethics Code to take action against a person's employment, advancement, or any opportunity merely as a result of being named by a complainant. Nothing in Standard 1.08 precludes such actions as long as the complaint itself is not the basis on which such decisions are made. In many instances, complaints are dismissed and the psychologist exonerated. In some instances, an agency or organization will receive information such as eyewitness testimony, relevant records, or even admission on the part of the psychologist, which may form the basis of appropriate adverse action. But, taking action against a person merely on the basis of an ethics complaint is inappropriate and unethical. If, after investigation, an ethics committee or licensing board finds a psychologist to be in violation of the Ethics Code, then specific actions bearing on employment, advancement, licensure, and other professional privileges may be appropriate.

Common Dilemmas and Conflicts

- It is very tempting to assume guilt when a person is named in an ethics complaint. But even when convinced of a complaint's validity, taking additional action against that individual prior to conclusion of an ethics investigation is a violation of the APA Ethics Code.
- Taking adverse action against the professional status or career of a person simply because he or she has named you or a colleague in a complaint is unethical.
- Those who violate this standard may simultaneously be in violation of employment law, stand in breech of contract, or face additional consequences.
- It may be tempting to take action against a colleague who files a complaint, but to do so is an abuse of power and a violation of this standard.

Prevention and Positive Practice

✓ Psychologists in positions of influence related to hiring, firing, admissions, promotion, and related professional status and advancement decisions should be fully aware of legal and ethical standards bearing on these decisions.
✓ Ensure due process in all such decisions, and never rush to judgment in the case of a colleague, supervisee, or student who has been named in an ethics complaint.

✓ Never base a job or promotion-related decision on evidence that a psychologist has filed an ethics complaint. Filing an ethics complaint when psychologists become aware of unethical behavior that cannot be resolved informally is an ethical mandate (Standard 1.05); taking action against a psychologist for fulfilling this obligation would undermine the Ethics Code.

✓ Employment, tenure, promotion, and related decisions can—and in most instances, should—be postponed pending the outcome and resolution of an ethics investigation. Of course information unrelated to the ethics complaint may serve as a basis for making such decisions.

✓ Outcomes of formal ethics committee proceedings may serve as legitimate reasons for making employment and advancement decisions about a student or psychologist.

Standard 2. Competence

2.01 Boundaries of Competence

   (a) Psychologists provide services, teach, and conduct research with populations and in areas only within the boundaries of their competence, based on their education, training, supervised experience, consultation, study, or professional experience.

   (b) Where scientific or professional knowledge in the discipline of psychology establishes that an understanding of factors associated with age, gender, gender identity, race, ethnicity, culture, national origin, religion, sexual orientation, disability, language, or socioeconomic status is essential for effective implementation of their services or research, psychologists have or obtain the training, experience, consultation, or supervision necessary to ensure the competence of their services, or they make appropriate referrals, except as provided in Standard 2.02, Providing Services in Emergencies.

   (c) Psychologists planning to provide services, teach, or conduct research involving populations, areas, techniques, or technologies new to them undertake relevant education, training, supervised experience, consultation, or study.

   (d) When psychologists are asked to provide services to individuals for whom appropriate mental health services are not available and for which psychologists have not obtained the competence necessary, psychologists with closely related prior training or experience may provide such services in order to ensure that services are not denied if they make a reasonable effort to obtain the competence required by using relevant research, training, consultation, or study.

(e) In those emerging areas in which generally recognized standards for preparatory training do not yet exist, psychologists nevertheless take reasonable steps to ensure the competence of their work and to protect clients/patients, students, supervisees, research participants, organizational clients, and others from harm.

(f) When assuming forensic roles, psychologists are or become reasonably familiar with the judicial or administrative rules governing their roles.

Essential Elements

Psychologists are ethically obligated to ensure their own competence. In most jurisdictions, this is also a legal requirement. Competence is defined as having the necessary knowledge, abilities, skills, and values to provide effective services. Competence does not mean perfection; a psychologist may be competent in one area and not in others. Additionally, one may be competent at one point in time and not at another, especially in light of the rapid accumulation of research and practice knowledge in psychology. A psychologist may have either *general competence* (skills common to most psychologists as a function of standard education and training in psychology) or *specialty competence* (skills requiring specialized training such as neuropsychiatric assessment or treatment of eating disorders), and it is imperative that one knows the difference. Competence falls along a continuum, and psychologists must work to enhance their own competence over their careers, making efforts to avoid degradation of knowledge and skills. Psychologists must remain sensitive to cultural diversity in those they serve, challenge personal biases, and continually work to update knowledge and skills related to diverse groups and the range of individual variation within those groups.

Common Dilemmas and Conflicts

- Academic degrees, licenses, and certifications can never guarantee that a psychologist is competent; psychologists cannot assume that their education or credentials necessarily make them competent with specific client types, disorders, or practice modalities.
- Offering services outside of one's areas of competence raises the probability of professional negligence and potential harm to clients.
- Psychologists who ignore or fail to recognize culturally relevant variables increase the risk of incompetent practice, biased or stereotypical responses, and discrimination against culturally different clients.
- Psychologists with inflated or unrealistic perceptions of their own competence are at risk in this area.
- Psychologists who fear the financial implications of referring current clients or who accept all referrals they receive are at risk in this area.
- Feeling overwhelmed, confused, or "stuck" regarding a specific case does not necessarily signal incompetence.
- Psychologists working in small or isolated communities frequently struggle with balancing competence and the clinical needs of persons who might otherwise go without services.
- At times, efforts to competently conform practice to a culturally different client's expectations (e.g., therapist self-disclosure, friendly hugs on greeting) may result in apparent conflicts with other portions of the Ethics Code.
- Academic psychologists and researchers must be alert to perceived pressures, demands, and conflicts of interest that may result in teaching outside their competence or engaging in fraudulent research activities.

Prevention and Positive Practice

- ✓ Competence is rooted in the principles of beneficence and nonmaleficence; above all, remember that ensuring your own competence is a way to protect those you serve.
- ✓ Do not decide whether you are competent to provide a particular service without consulting an experienced colleague with expertise in that area.

✓ If you are uncomfortable with colleagues knowing that you are providing a particular service, you should probably not be offering it.

✓ Remember the competence criteria most peers and licensing boards will apply; ask an established expert in the practice area you are considering whether you have the education, professional training, and supervised experience necessary for competent practice.

✓ When attempting to establish competence in an area of professional practice:

- review all relevant guidelines for education, training, and supervision;
- seek formal training or certification programs in that area;
- consult with a recognized expert;
- obtain appropriate applied experience supervised by an acknowledged expert in that area;
- make a joint decision with that expert regarding whether you are ready to practice independently in that area;
- obtain ongoing consultation with an experienced colleague as needed; and
- be sure to maintain competence through ongoing continuing education activities.

✓ Refuse to accept client referrals or assignments to practice areas in which you do not have established competence.

✓ When existing clients manifest problems or require services for which you do not have established competence, refer them to a competent provider.

✓ Practice making skillful referrals when the limits of your competence are reached, ensuring that clients understand the reason for the referral and feel neither rejected nor abandoned.

✓ Arrange for ongoing and active peer consultation—peer consultation groups may be especially helpful—and invite honest input regarding your competence with specific problems or client types.

✓ When practicing outside your competence because no competent colleague is available within a reasonable distance, work actively to expand and improve your competence through education, self-study, supervision, and consultation, making use of all available technologies.

✓ Although competence in working with individuals of diverse backgrounds is an essential aspect of psychologists' general competence, competence in this area should be enhanced by
- actively seeking opportunities for education, training, and supervision in service delivery to culturally diverse groups;
- actively incorporating the full range of individual differences and cultural differences into client intakes and ongoing service delivery, even in areas that are not readily apparent;
- carefully considering demographic variables before selecting assessment instruments or determining a treatment plan;
- framing individual differences as possible sources of strength and therapeutic resources;
- remaining vigilant to personal biases and actively consulting with colleagues when your cultural competence may be exceeded; and
- developing a network of community resources for consultation, collaboration, and referral (e.g., clergy; bilingual colleagues; experts in gay, lesbian, bisexual, transsexual, and transgender issues).

✓ Be cognizant of relevant research and practice guidelines bearing on work with diverse clients. Although not enforceable standards, it may be useful to occasionally review the American Psychological Association's (APA's)
- Guidelines on Multicultural Education, Training, Research, Practice, and Organizational Change for Psychologists;
- Guidelines for Providers of Psychological Services to Ethnic, Linguistic, and Culturally Diverse Populations;
- Guidelines for Psychotherapy With Lesbian, Gay, and Bisexual Adults;
- Guidelines for Child Custody Evaluations in Divorce Proceedings;
- Guidelines for Practice With Older Adults; and
- Guidelines for Ethical Conduct in the Care and Use of Animals.

✓ Remember that emotional (interpersonal) competence is just as significant as knowledge based on technical competence.

✓ In general, avoid forensic work altogether unless you have specific supervised experience and thorough judicial and administrative knowledge in this area.

2.02 Providing Services in Emergencies

In emergencies, when psychologists provide services to individuals for whom other mental health services are not available and for which psychologists have not obtained the necessary training, psychologists may provide such services in order to ensure that services are not denied. The services are discontinued as soon as the emergency has ended or appropriate services are available.

Essential Elements

At times psychologists provide services in areas with limited professional resources such as rural areas, the military, or in remote or isolated locales. In these situations potential clients may have presenting problems outside the psychologist's areas of expertise. Although psychologists practicing in other circumstances would typically make a referral, finding an appropriately trained colleague in isolated settings may not be possible. In such situations, if the psychologist does not provide the needed services the client will likely go without treatment. Balancing beneficence with nonmaleficence results in the need to use one's general competence to provide the needed services while simultaneously developing one's competence in the more specialized areas relevant to the client's treatment needs. Such activities might include reading relevant professional literature, completing continuing education and other training activities, seeking ongoing clinical supervision, consulting with colleagues with expertise in the specialty area, and making use of all available technologies such as completing online continuing education courses and consulting with expert colleagues via telephone or e-mail.

Common Dilemmas and Conflicts

■ Psychologists who are overconfident that their "generalist" competence will suffice for most clients, problems, and interventions are at risk in this area.

- Lack of awareness of local colleagues and their areas of expertise may increase the risk of perceived need to provide emergency services outside of one's area of competence.
- Psychologists who fail to use all available colleagues when considering making referrals—including those in allied health professions—are at risk in this area.
- Psychologists who attempt to determine when client needs exceed their clinical capabilities without appropriate consultation are at risk in this area.
- When psychologists underestimate the training, consultation, or supervision needed to assist clients, they may neglect efforts to build appropriate competence when functioning outside their competence areas in emergencies.
- Problems arise when a psychologist providing emergency services to a client continues providing such services even after the emergency resolves or when a provider with appropriate expertise becomes available.

Prevention and Positive Practice

✓ Become aware of all treatment resources in your local area before the need to use them arises. Consider all other health professionals and allied health professionals, regardless of their professional discipline, as well as the clergy.

✓ Develop your expertise in using technology such as the Internet, e-mail, professional e-mail lists, and the like, to access colleagues outside of your local area.

✓ Compile a list of resources such as online continuing education providers, training opportunities available through local colleges and universities, and experts in various areas of practice with whom you may consult.

✓ Purchase access to online journal services such as PsycExtra, PsycINFO, and PsycARTICLES, which are available through the APA, for ready access to the professional literature.

✓ Obtain training in crisis management, assessment, and treatment of suicidal clients, and in other areas where emergencies and crises often arise. Try to develop solid generalist skills by seeking supervised experience with different groups such as children, adolescents, elderly persons, and others.

2.03 Maintaining Competence

Psychologists undertake ongoing efforts to develop and maintain their competence.

Essential Elements

Competence must be actively maintained, updated, and developed; resting on one's laurels places clients at risk. It is well known that over time psychologists may forget some of what they have learned; skills not used regularly may grow rusty; and the knowledge base needed for current and effective practice quickly expands. Failure to continually update one's knowledge and skills raises the risk of professional incompetence and potential harm to clients. Although many states require mandatory continuing education as part of the licensure renewal process, meeting these minimal requirements may be insufficient for maintaining competence.

Common Dilemmas and Conflicts

- Because knowledge becomes outdated, techniques antiquated, and seldom used skills atrophy, psychologists must be quite sensitive to the issue of degradation in their own competence.
- Trying to specialize in too many areas of practice may make genuine mastery of any area elusive.
- Those practicing in relative isolation may be unaware of new developments and practice standards in their field.
- Merely meeting minimal requirements for continuing education and licensure renewal may be insufficient for assuring sufficient levels of competence.

Prevention and Positive Practice

✓ Conduct an honest appraisal of your areas of competence as well as training or supervision needs on a regular basis. Seek input from trusted and respected colleagues with expertise in the area(s) of practice in question.
✓ Actively consult practice guidelines, research findings, and the relevant literature. Determine how much and what type of additional training will be needed to maintain a high

level of competence in those areas in which you practice (see the Appendix [Key Ethics Resources for Psychologists], this volume).

✓ Frame continuing education requirements as minimal standards and actively seek out the education and training needed to remain competent in all areas in which you practice.

✓ Subscribe to and read peer reviewed journals relevant to the work you do; for instance, clinicians might consider the *Clinician's Research Digest* and *Professional Psychology: Research and Practice*.

✓ Join professional associations relevant to your work focus, and participate in committee work and e-mail list discussions. If they offer a mentoring program, consider joining to receive the benefits of a mentor with relevant expertise.

✓ Consider the board certification process through the American Board of Professional Psychology to obtain feedback from expert peers on your clinical competence.

✓ Intentional development and maintenance of competence must be a perpetual attitude and professional commitment. Keep in mind that ensuring your own competence is central to achieving the aspirational ideals of the APA Ethics Code's General Principles.

2.04 Bases for Scientific and Professional Judgments

Psychologists' work is based on established scientific and professional knowledge of the discipline. (See also Standards 2.01e, Boundaries of Competence, and 10.01b, Informed Consent to Therapy.)

Essential Elements

Psychologists are obligated to base their assessments, interventions, and public statements on established knowledge in the field of psychology. In other words, psychologists should know what instruments and interventions to use in specific circumstances with specific persons, and they should know why they are using them. Always keeping their clients' best interests in view, psychologists emphasize both evidence-based knowledge and prevailing professional standards; psychologists avoid approaches for which no substantive scientific or professional rationale exists.

Common Dilemmas and Conflicts

- Psychologists who lack appropriate training, experience, and supervision in an area are more likely to operate outside the boundaries of scientific and professional knowledge in that area.
- Those who practice "fringe" or atypical assessment and intervention approaches are at greater risk for problems in this area.
- Psychologists who offer a purely theoretical versus an evidence-based rationale for their work are at greater risk for problems in this area.
- Psychologists who distance themselves from colleagues— perhaps on the basis of theoretical differences—and eschew peer review and consultation are at greater risk for problems in this area.

Prevention and Positive Practice

- ✓ Be a student of the scholarly literature in the field of psychology generally and in your areas of practice specifically.
- ✓ When engaging in professional work of any kind, ask yourself: "What would a jury of my peers have to say about the basis of my work?"
- ✓ Engage in a regular peer consultation group and solicit feedback about the appropriateness of your professional work in light of existing research and professional knowledge; make sure to include peers who do not share your theoretical approach.
- ✓ Occasionally revisit continuing education material, case notes, class lecture materials, and published work and ensure that your work is rooted in current and credible scientific and professional evidence.

2.05 Delegation of Work to Others

Psychologists who delegate work to employees, supervisees, or research or teaching assistants or who use the

services of others, such as interpreters, take reasonable steps to (1) avoid delegating such work to persons who have a multiple relationship with those being served that would likely lead to exploitation or loss of objectivity; (2) authorize only those responsibilities that such persons can be expected to perform competently on the basis of their education, training, or experience, either independently or with the level of supervision being provided; and (3) see that such persons perform these services competently. (See also Standards 2.02, Providing Services in Emergencies; 3.05, Multiple Relationships; 4.01, Maintaining Confidentiality; 9.01, Bases for Assessments; 9.02, Use of Assessments; 9.03, Informed Consent in Assessments; and 9.07, Assessment by Unqualified Persons.)

Essential Elements

Psychologists frequently work with supervisees, junior associates, teaching and research assistants, office staff, and others in the course of their professional activities. Psychologists are responsible for the quality of work done by subordinates, must not delegate any tasks that are outside the boundaries of their competence or their professional role, must supervise subordinates adequately to ensure they are providing services appropriately and competently, and must ensure that all delegated tasks are appropriate for the individuals involved. Before delegating any task, the psychologist should ensure that the subordinate does not have any conflict of interest or multiple relationships that might adversely impact his or her objectivity or judgment. It is also important to ensure that all tasks that are delegated are consistent with the role and training of the subordinate, such as not authorizing a secretary or receptionist to administer and interpret psychological tests. Psychologists must keep in mind that they hold the ultimate responsibility for the client's welfare and for the quality of work provided by subordinates. Although some tasks and professional functions may be appropriately delegated to subordinates, this should be done with care, forethought, and sufficient supervision to ensure that standards of care are not jeopardized.

Common Dilemmas and Conflicts

- Psychologists who rely too much on trainees, supervisees, and other subordinates to provide clinical services are at increased risk of having harm occur to clients and others.
- Psychologists experiencing financial pressures and the need for greater income may be motivated to overuse subordinates.
- Failure to assess subordinates' actual competence prior to delegating tasks or leaving it up to subordinates to assess their own competence may suggest incompetent delegation. It is tempting but usually erroneous to assume that subordinates have knowledge or skills equivalent to the psychologist's own.
- Providing cursory or insufficient supervision based on the nature of the tasks being delegated and/or the subordinate's actual training needs is a recipe for difficulty in this area.
- Psychologists who fail to make arrangements to be available for emergency consultation with subordinates should problems arise are at greater risk in this area.

Prevention and Positive Practice

✓ Before delegating any tasks to subordinates, first assess their competence to carry out the desired tasks. Provide them with the needed training and supervise them actively enough to ensure competence.

✓ Engage in an informed consent agreement with subordinates that includes tasks involved, supervisory arrangements, evaluation criteria, methods for delivering feedback and training, ethical requirements, and avenues for addressing grievances.

✓ Ensure that subordinates understand the limits of their roles and competence and that they practice within parameters agreed on in advance.

✓ Clarify the roles of all subordinates with all clients in advance, delineating limits of confidentiality, and ensure that subordinates do not misrepresent their credentials or roles.

✓ Instruct subordinates not only in clinical areas but in ethics and legal issues as well. For instance, be sure that they understand the limits of their roles and relevant issues such as confidentiality, boundaries, and multiple relationships.

✓ Accept full responsibility for all services provided by subordinates. Doing so will increase your attention to providing necessary supervision and ongoing training.

✓ Promote the well-being of supervisees and employees by improving their job skills, enhancing their work environment, and building on their strengths.

2.06 Personal Problems and Conflicts

(a) Psychologists refrain from initiating an activity when they know or should know that there is a substantial likelihood that their personal problems will prevent them from performing their work-related activities in a competent manner.

(b) When psychologists become aware of personal problems that may interfere with their performing work-related duties adequately, they take appropriate measures, such as obtaining professional consultation or assistance, and determine whether they should limit, suspend, or terminate their work-related duties. (See also Standard 10.10, Terminating Therapy.)

Essential Elements

Psychologists are human. In addition to the full range of normal life stressors and challenges, psychologists face the added stress of working with impaired and emotionally demanding clients, many of whom may relapse or not improve. Psychologists may experience occasional distress, burnout, and impaired competence. Some psychologists bring problematic personal histories or personality characteristics to their work, and still others suffer from professional blind spots as caregivers and fail to recognize personal distress or professional impairment. For these reasons, psychologists must remain vigilant to the impact of distress, burnout, and vicarious traumatization on their ability to function effectively. To avoid harm to clients and to ensure competent professional work, psychologists must take steps to remain self-aware and connected to colleagues who are willing to both confront and assist them when personal problems and conflicts interfere with competence.

Common Dilemmas and Conflicts

- Psychologists who ignore, minimize, or rationalize signs of distress or impairment are at increased risk for problems in this area.
- When psychologists equate help-seeking with weakness or incompetence, they are at increased risk for problems in this area.
- The lower a psychologist's level of familiarity with personal vulnerabilities and weaknesses, the greater the probability of difficulty in this area.
- Psychologists experiencing personal problems and emotional distress are at increased risk for boundary violations (Standard 3.05) and termination difficulties (Standard 10.10) with clients.
- Problems arise when psychologists begin seeking to get their own needs met by or through clients and yet fail to seek appropriate assistance.
- Psychologists who keep concerns about distress, burnout, or impairment to themselves are at increased risk in this area.

Prevention and Positive Practice

- ✓ First, admit you are vulnerable to distress and impairment, in other words, a human being.
- ✓ Make a commitment to promoting and maintaining your own emotional, physical, relational, and spiritual health. For instance, actively engage in routine exercise, adequate sleep, healthy eating, leisure activities, and social relationships.
- ✓ Maintain a balance between your professional and personal life, and set firm boundaries between the two.
- ✓ In addition to routine daily breaks, take longer breaks in the form of half or full days off periodically as well as regular vacation time.
- ✓ Know your limits; set firm boundaries—and stick to them—when it comes to the number of clients you will see and the number of hours you will work.
- ✓ When possible, engage in a multifaceted practice; within your weekly time constraints seek a range of professional activities (e.g., assessment, counseling, teaching, supervision, consultation).

✓ Be alert to personal distress or red flags such as increased boredom, anger, or irritability with clients; decreased empathy; wishing you were elsewhere during sessions; canceling appointments; or fantasizing frequently about a client.

✓ When red flags emerge, seek consultation from a trusted colleague and with necessary consultation and supervision, decide what steps you should take.

✓ Actively arrange and participate in a peer supervision or support group. Openly discuss personal problems, professional challenges, and work stressors.

✓ Participate in your own personal psychotherapy at various times throughout your career as you face different life transitions and challenges.

✓ Avoid negative coping behaviors such as substance abuse, overeating, sleep deprivation, or withdrawal from relationships.

✓ Strive for psychological health and wellness; engage in ongoing self-care activities that promote your effective functioning.

Standard 3. Human Relations

3.01 Unfair Discrimination

In their work-related activities, psychologists do not engage in unfair discrimination based on age, gender, gender identity, race, ethnicity, culture, national origin, religion, sexual orientation, disability, socioeconomic status, or any basis proscribed by law.

Essential Elements

It is vital that psychologists—through any act or omission—avoid any form of unfair discrimination. This standard, built on the definition of diversity provided in Principle E: Respect for People's Rights and Dignity, states very clearly that psychologists should never discriminate against another individual on the basis of any of the individual differences that comprise diversity. Discrimination would also violate the ideals espoused in Principles A (Beneficence and Nonmaleficence) and D (Justice). Such discrimination constitutes an abuse of psychologists' power, would likely result in harm, and is antithetical to the profession's commitment to a respect for individual differences as well as caring and concern for all individuals. Further, psychologists are not limited by the individual differences listed in this standard. They are guided to respect all individual differences and to work against discrimination in all their work settings.

Common Dilemmas and Conflicts

- Psychologists who harbor either overt or unconscious stereotyped or biased views of specific groups of people are at greater risk in this area.
- Although *direct discrimination* (overt differential treatment based on arbitrary factors) is easy to detect, *indirect discrimination* is subtler, equally harmful, and more difficult to address.
- If a psychologist consistently makes services available for, grants resources to, or creates other advantages for certain groups at the expense of others, unfair discrimination may be present.
- When psychologists fail to consider the validity of assessment practices for specific groups, unfair discrimination is more likely to occur.

Prevention and Positive Practice

- ✓ First, seek self-awareness—through reflection, education, and consultation with regard to feelings and beliefs about diverse groups. If biases are revealed, embark on a program of remediation.
- ✓ Honestly evaluate the extent to which members of diverse groups have equal access to your services as clinician, educator, or consultant.
- ✓ Carefully consider the outcomes of your work; if in hiring, promoting, grading, or providing treatment, certain groups consistently receive better outcomes than others, explore the reasons why.
- ✓ Do not tolerate stereotyped views or discriminatory practices in the organizations or settings in which you work.
- ✓ Find creative ways to promote inclusion and acceptance (e.g., place culturally diverse or stereotype-incongruent artwork in your waiting room).
- ✓ Remain fully cognizant of laws and regulations bearing on unfair discrimination. For example, be familiar with your obligations under the Americans With Disabilities Act (http://www.usdoj.gov/crt/ada/adahom1.htm).

3.02 Sexual Harassment

Psychologists do not engage in sexual harassment. Sexual harassment is sexual solicitation, physical advances, or verbal or nonverbal conduct that is sexual in nature, that occurs in connection with the psychologist's activities or roles as a psychologist, and that either (1) is unwelcome, is offensive, or creates a hostile workplace or educational environment, and the psychologist knows or is told this or (2) is sufficiently severe or intense to be abusive to a reasonable person in the context. Sexual harassment can consist of a single intense or severe act or of multiple persistent or pervasive acts. (See also Standard 1.08, Unfair Discrimination Against Complainants and Respondents.)

Essential Elements

This standard provides a succinct definition of sexual harassment and further elucidates that psychologists never engage in sexual harassment. Psychologists should be sensitive to the impact of their actions on others and vigilant to the varied ways in which their words and behaviors may be interpreted. Sexually demeaning or assaultive behavior is always out-of-bounds for psychologists. Even if their actions carry no ill intent, if advised that they are offensive, they should cease them immediately. They are also responsible to know which actions and behaviors are likely to be perceived as abusive by the average person and not engage in them at any time.

Common Dilemmas and Conflicts

- Psychologists lacking in self-awareness, maturity, emotional intelligence, and good collegial support are at greater risk in this area.
- Psychologists suffering from loneliness, relationship dysfunction, mood problems, and phase-of-life turmoil are at greater risk in this area.
- Personal entitlement, assumptions about sexual access to those with whom psychologists work, or discomfort with nonsexual intimate relationships may underlie some instances of sexual harassment.

■ Licensing boards and ethics committees are likely to uphold an extremely rigorous standard in this area: Sexual harassment will never be tolerated.

Prevention and Positive Practice

✓ Be exceptionally cautious about any comment or behavior that could possibly be construed by any reasonable person as sexually provocative, degrading, or coercive.

✓ Avoid making any sexually explicit attempts at humor; assume that your humorous intent will be misconstrued.

✓ Never condone sexually inappropriate behavior in employees, supervisees, students, and colleagues; address it immediately.

✓ Remain open and responsive to feedback from colleagues and clients; when another person brings potentially harassing behavior to your attention, immediately cease and desist.

3.03 Other Harassment

Psychologists do not knowingly engage in behavior that is harassing or demeaning to persons with whom they interact in their work based on factors such as those persons' age, gender, gender identity, race, ethnicity, culture, national origin, religion, sexual orientation, disability, language, or socioeconomic status.

Essential Elements

In addition to the requirements not to discriminate against others on the basis of any of these individual differences (Standard 3.01) or engage in sexual harassment of others in their professional roles (Standard 3.02), psychologists may not knowingly engage in any other form of harassing or demeaning behavior. Psychologists must demonstrate respect for individual differences, an obligation that diminishes the probability of harassment. They should be vigilant to demeaning behavior that may be subtle and unintended. If ever informed that in spite of these efforts psychologists have demeaned or harassed another person, they should remedy this immediately.

Common Dilemmas and Conflicts

- Psychologists who lack experience with or sensitivity to individuals who are different in terms of any diversity variable are at greater risk in this area.
- Psychologists who hold stereotypical views of or biases toward specific groups or lack genuine cross-cultural empathy are at greater risk in this area.
- Licensing boards and ethics committees are likely to uphold an extremely rigorous standard in this area: Harassment or demeaning behavior of any kind can be expected to trigger a very serious response.

Prevention and Positive Practice

- ✓ Carefully avoid any comment or behavior that could be construed as disparaging or demeaning to persons of any age, gender, gender identity, race, ethnicity, culture, national origin, religion, sexual orientation, disability, language, or socioeconomic status.
- ✓ Immediately address harassing or demeaning behavior in employees, supervisees, and students.
- ✓ Remain open and responsive to feedback from colleagues and clients; when another person brings potentially harassing behavior to your attention, immediately cease and desist.

3.04 Avoiding Harm

Psychologists take reasonable steps to avoid harming their clients/patients, students, supervisees, research participants, organizational clients, and others with whom they work, and to minimize harm where it is foreseeable and unavoidable.

Essential Elements

Consistent with General Principle A (Beneficence and Non-maleficence), psychologists must actively work to prevent harm from occurring to anyone with whom they interact professionally. In many ways, this standard is fundamental to everything else in the Ethics Code. They must proactively anticipate the possibility of harm and take preventative steps to minimize the chance of it occurring. Psychologists are responsible for show-ing intentional and thoughtful efforts to prevent harm to those touched by their professional work. When harm is possible or unavoidable, psychologists must actively work to minimize it.

Common Dilemmas and Conflicts

- Psychologists who lose sight of the need to avoid harm or who place their own interests before those with whom they work are at greater risk in this area.
- Failure to consider the potential for adverse outcomes of one's services may signal inexperience, carelessness, or incompetence.
- At times, therapeutic interventions, research protocols, or educational experiences necessitate some level of dis-comfort, distress, or even pain. The key is whether the psy-chologist anticipated these concerns, took reasonable steps to minimize them, and provided thorough informed con-sent to participants.

Prevention and Positive Practice

- ✓ Keep the ancient wisdom of the Hippocratic oath in mind in all of your professional activities: "Abstain from what-ever is harmful or mischievous."
- ✓ Before developing a treatment plan, creating a research pro-tocol, or designing any educational experience, carefully consider the range of potential responses and the probabil-ity of harm.
- ✓ Consult with colleagues when you are unclear about the possible adverse effects of any professional activity; demon-strate reasonable steps to both anticipate and prevent harm.
- ✓ If unforeseeable harm becomes evident, inform those harmed by your activities; take immediate steps to stop fur-ther harm; and seek consultation regarding the most appro-priate way to ameliorate the problem and benefit those with whom you work.

3.05 Multiple Relationships

(a) **A multiple relationship occurs when a psychologist is in a professional role with a person and (1) at the** same time is in another role with the same person, (2) at the same time is in a relationship with a person closely associated with or related to the person with whom the psychologist has the professional relationship, or (3) promises to enter into another relationship in the future with the person or a person closely associated with or related to the person.

A psychologist refrains from entering into a multiple relationship if the multiple relationship could reasonably be expected to impair the psychologist's objectivity, competence, or effectiveness in performing his or her functions as a psychologist, or otherwise risks exploitation or harm to the person with whom the professional relationship exists.

Multiple relationships that would not reasonably be expected to cause impairment or risk exploitation or harm are not unethical.

(b) If a psychologist finds that, due to unforeseen factors, a potentially harmful multiple relationship has arisen, the psychologist takes reasonable steps to resolve it with due regard for the best interests of the affected person and maximal compliance with the Ethics Code.

(c) When psychologists are required by law, institutional policy, or extraordinary circumstances to serve in more than one role in judicial or administrative proceedings, at the outset they clarify role expectations and the extent of confidentiality and thereafter as changes occur. (See also Standards 3.04, Avoiding Harm, and 3.07, Third-Party Requests for Services.)

Essential Elements

Psychologists are directed to exercise caution when considering entering into multiple relationships, defined as being in a professional relationship with an individual along with a personal or other nonprofessional relationship, doing the same with a significant other of that individual, or stating or implying an intention to enter into a different kind of relationship following termination of the professional one. This standard does not prohibit all multiple relationships, and it does not suggest that all role blending is necessarily harmful. However, if there is a reasonable likelihood of impaired objectivity, poor judgment, or diminished competence, or if the likelihood of exploitation or harm to the other individual is significant, then psychologists are to avoid such multiple relationships. If a psychologist discovers the presence of a multiple relationship that is likely to be potentially harmful, efforts must be made to resolve the matter without causing any further harm to that individual. For those psychologists serving in settings that require engaging in more than one role with an individual (e.g., forensic assessment, military psychology, rural communities) it is essential to clarify role expectations and the extent of confidentiality both at the outset and thereafter as changes occur.

Common Dilemmas and Conflicts

- Psychologists with less training and experience or difficulty with personal boundaries are at greater risk for engaging in inappropriate multiple relationships.
- As role blending increases, a psychologist's objectivity and efficacy may decline, and those served become more vulnerable to exploitation.
- Although psychologists must avoid porous boundaries and harmful multiple relationships, they must simultaneously avoid becoming so rigid and relationally sterile that the efficacy of their services is diminished.
- Because of the inherent power differential between psychologists and clients, nonprofessional relationships with current or former clients are unlikely to be truly mutual and may be confusing for both parties.
- At times, crossing traditional boundaries (e.g., meeting location, touch, self-disclosure, gift exchange) may be culturally or therapeutically indicated.
- Harmful multiple relationships increase in probability when a psychologist works with clients with poor interpersonal boundaries, personality disorders, or a history of exploitative relationships as well as when a psychologist is suffering distress or relationship dysfunction.

Prevention and Positive Practice

✓ Remember that caution about multiple relationships should emanate from an interest in benefiting and protecting those with whom we work.

✓ Sexual or romantic relationships with those we serve professionally are always forbidden.

✓ Before embarking on a second (nonprofessional) relationship with an individual to whom you provide professional services, ask yourself several questions:

  ▪ What options and alternatives to entering the secondary relationship exist? Can the client's needs be met without the additional relationship?

  ▪ Is entering the secondary relationship consistent with the client's treatment needs, the agreed on goals of treatment, and prevailing professional standards?

  ▪ Is there any potential for the secondary relationship to harm the person?

  ▪ Might the secondary relationship undermine the trust or dependence on you?

  ▪ Is there any chance that the secondary relationship could impair objectivity, create conflicts of interest, or lead to exploitation?

✓ Seek consultation from an experienced colleague before entering or continuing in a secondary relationship; consider the possibility that your objectivity in the matter is already compromised.

✓ Work to balance good boundaries with the unique therapeutic needs and cultural expectations of clients; document your rationale and any consultations as you navigate these concerns.

✓ When working in a setting in which multiple relationships are unavoidable, demonstrate extra attention to informed consent (Standards 3.10 and 10.01) and confidentiality (Standard 4).

3.06 Conflict of Interest

Psychologists refrain from taking on a professional role when personal, scientific, professional, legal, financial, or other interests or relationships could reasonably be expected to (1) impair their objectivity, competence, or effectiveness in performing their functions as psychologists or (2) expose the person or organization with whom the professional relationship exists to harm or exploitation.

Essential Elements

Just as psychologists should avoid potentially problematic multiple relationships (Standard 3.05), they should avoid situations in which the best interests of those they serve are likely to be compromised by competing interests (e.g., financial benefit to the psychologist, existing relationships). Psychologists should not enter into relationships that would create a conflict of interest in which their objectivity, judgment, competence, or effectiveness might be diminished or where the other individual might be exposed to harm. If there is a reasonable probability that a psychologist will not be able to remain objective because of another personal, scientific, professional, or financial relationship, then the psychologist should avoid entering into a professional relationship because of the potential for harm to the other person. Psychologists should consider all reasonably available options and alternatives prior to entering into relationships or roles that present such conflicts of interest.

Common Dilemmas and Conflicts

- In many instances, relationships with clients, students, and others are already imbalanced with respect to power; psychologists are vulnerable to exploiting this imbalance when their own interests (e.g., financial, vocational, social) are at odds with those of the people they serve.
- Psychologists working in corporations, for the government, or with health maintenance organizations (HMOs) are especially vulnerable to discovering that their personal financial or career status may be threatened by placing a client's best interests first.
- Even well-intended psychologists may be less objective and fair in determining others' best interests when these conflict with their own.

Prevention and Positive Practice

- ✓ Cautiously avoiding inappropriate multiple relationships with those you serve will simultaneously help reduce the risk of conflicts of interest.
- ✓ When working for or through a third party (e.g., HMO, government agency), clarify your obligation to protect the interests of those you serve.

✓ Provide full and continuous disclosure to those you serve regarding your obligations to third parties.

✓ Be cautious about being inadvertently co-opted by a third party that has power over your livelihood, yet which may not share the same focus on the best interests of those you serve.

✓ If a conflict between the interests of someone you serve and your own interests becomes risky or problematic, consider referring the client with due consideration of his or her best interests.

3.07 Third-Party Requests for Services

When psychologists agree to provide services to a person or entity at the request of a third party, psychologists attempt to clarify at the outset of the service the nature of the relationship with all individuals or organizations involved. This clarification includes the role of the psychologist (e.g., therapist, consultant, diagnostician, or expert witness), an identification of who is the client, the probable uses of the services provided or the information obtained, and the fact that there may be limits to confidentiality. (See also Standards 3.05, Multiple Relationships, and 4.02, Discussing the Limits of Confidentiality.)

Essential Elements

It is not always the psychologist's client who contracts for professional services. When a third party (e.g., parent, guardian, employer, court) requests that a psychologist provide services to another individual, heightened attention is required to ensure that all expectations and parameters regarding the professional relationship are clarified and agreed on prior to any service delivery. What are the psychologist's specific roles and duties? Who is the client? How will information obtained in the professional relationship be used? Are any limits to confidentiality anticipated based on the presence of a third party? If so, these must be clarified in advance to avoid misunderstandings and to prevent any harm from occurring to the client(s). By clarifying roles and other expectations in advance, and with both parties, the potential for role conflict and unmet expectations may be substantially diminished and the likelihood of harm may be minimized.

Common Dilemmas and Conflicts

- Quite often, the kinds of events that trigger a third-party request for services (e.g., criminal charges, substance-related incidents, poor work performance, custody disputes) often indicate incongruent agendas on the part of the client and the third party.
- Differing expectations may be present regarding the use or control of information shared with the psychologist.
- When a third party refers a person for psychological services, the psychologist may discover hidden agendas on the part of the referral source, resistance on the part of the client, and weighty consequences bearing on the psychologist's work.

Prevention and Positive Practice

- ✓ Immediately clarify the identity of the primary client.
- ✓ Clarify your obligations to each party prior to providing any services through clear informed consent that includes limits of confidentiality and how the results of your assessment or intervention may be used, including potentially negative consequences.
- ✓ Inform those you serve about their right to decline participation.
- ✓ Obligations to third parties never reduce your obligations to avoid harm and benefit those you serve.
- ✓ If a third-party request conflicts with your obligations to protect individuals from harm, respectfully decline the request.

3.08 Exploitative Relationships

Psychologists do not exploit persons over whom they have supervisory, evaluative, or other authority such as clients/patients, students, supervisees, research participants, and employees. (See also Standards 3.05, Multiple Relationships; 6.04, Fees and Financial Arrangements; 6.05, Barter With Clients/Patients; 7.07, Sexual Relationships With Students and Supervisees; 10.05, Sexual Intimacies With Current Therapy Clients/Patients; 10.06, Sexual Intimacies With Relatives or Significant Others of Current Therapy Clients/Patients; 10.07, Therapy With Former Sexual Partners; and 10.08, Sexual Intimacies With Former Therapy Clients/Patients.)

Essential Elements

Exploitation is the selfish utilization of another person for personal gain. Regardless of one's professional role, be it psychotherapist, supervisor, researcher, teacher, employer, or other, psychologists do not take advantage of the power inherent in these roles or violate the trust others place in them. Engaging in any actions that result in exploitation of those psychologists serve would be contrary to their essential obligations in Principle A (Beneficence and Nonmaleficence). Multiple relationships (Standard 3.05) and conflicts of interest (Standard 3.06) significantly increase the risk of exploitation. Courts and ethics committees typically consider the exploitation of a consumer's trust or dependency to be gross negligence. Psychologists should avoid professional relationships in which there is a reasonably high risk for exploitation and recognize that power differences—although frequently invisible—heighten the risk of exploitation.

Common Dilemmas and Conflicts

- The greater the role blending with a client, student, or supervisee and the greater the potential for a conflict of interest with that person, the greater the risk that the client or student will be objectified and serve as a source of gratification for the psychologist.
- Psychologists often rationalize reasons for engaging in exploitive relationships (e.g., it was beneficial to the client; it was unavoidable; it was mutual); none of these reasons will be compelling to a regulatory body.
- Psychologists always occupy positions of power relative to consumers and are therefore accorded substantial trust; even when a psychologist experiences a relationship with a client, student, or supervisee as egalitarian and mutual, there are often subtle power differences and dependency dynamics, and therefore there is vulnerability to exploitation.

Prevention and Positive Practice

✓ Be very cautious about multiple relationships (Standard 3.05) and alert to potential conflicts of interest (Standard 3.06).

✓ Assume that you have greater power than every person with whom you work professionally; consider their best interests in all you do.

✓ Although romantic and sexual relationships with clients and students are always considered exploitative, remember that exploitation can also be harmful even if more subtle (e.g., academic—coercing work from students, emotional—fueled by excessive self-disclosure and loneliness, or financial—accepting lavish gifts).

✓ When tempted to take some personal advantage of a professional relationship, assume that you hold greater power, that the person is vulnerable, and that your judgment may be compromised by the potential gain; seek consultation before proceeding.

3.09 Cooperation With Other Professionals

When indicated and professionally appropriate, psychologists cooperate with other professionals in order to serve their clients/patients effectively and appropriately. (See also Standard 4.05, Disclosures.)

Essential Elements

Some individuals receive services from more than one professional, either simultaneously or over time. Psychologists must respond in a timely, thoughtful, and helpful way when requests for information are received from either clients—current or former—or other professionals. Of course, psychologists must ensure that appropriate authorization has been granted first. If cooperating with a request from another professional may be harmful to the client or somehow not professionally appropriate, psychologists should share their concerns about the client's best interest and work with clients to achieve a resolution in accordance with the client's rights.

Common Dilemmas and Conflicts

■ A psychologist who ignores requests from other professionals or who excessively delays responding may be in violation of the Ethics Code.

- Psychologists prone to annoyance, anger, or arrogance are at greater risk for passive-aggressive refusals to cooperate with other professionals.
- Psychologists with negative or stereotyped views of other professional groups (e.g., counselors, physicians, social workers, lawyers) are at greater risk of failing to cooperate effectively.
- Psychologists with unresolved anger at former clients for terminating treatment, jealousy for other professionals, shame regarding poor service delivery, or fear that something in their relationship with the client will be revealed may be at increased risk in this area.

Prevention and Positive Practice

✓ Be attentive to every request from another professional and respond in a courteous and timely fashion—even if you must cordially request evidence of appropriate authorization to release information or decline the request because of its inappropriate nature (e.g., a pastor requests raw test data).

✓ If tempted to ignore a request from another professional, examine your motivations for doing so; consider your ethical obligations to the client and the impact of an unprofessional response on the public image of psychology.

✓ Remember that cooperation with other professionals is not about you. Cooperation is mandated so that professionals can work for the benefit of those served.

✓ Always keep the best interests of your clients and former clients in mind when making decisions in response to such requests.

3.10 Informed Consent

(a) When psychologists conduct research or provide assessment, therapy, counseling, or consulting services in person or via electronic transmission or other forms of communication, they obtain the informed consent of the individual or individuals using language that is reasonably understandable to that person or persons except when conducting such activities without consent is mandated by law or governmental regulation or as otherwise provided in this Ethics Code. (See also Standards 8.02,

Informed Consent to Research; 9.03, Informed Consent in Assessments; and 10.01, Informed Consent to Therapy.)

(b) For persons who are legally incapable of giving informed consent, psychologists nevertheless (1) provide an appropriate explanation, (2) seek the individual's assent, (3) consider such persons' preferences and best interests, and (4) obtain appropriate permission from a legally authorized person, if such substitute consent is permitted or required by law. When consent by a legally authorized person is not permitted or required by law, psychologists take reasonable steps to protect the individual's rights and welfare.

(c) When psychological services are court ordered or otherwise mandated, psychologists inform the individual of the nature of the anticipated services, including whether the services are court ordered or mandated and any limits of confidentiality, before proceeding.

(d) Psychologists appropriately document written or oral consent, permission, and assent. (See also Standards 8.02, Informed Consent to Research; 9.03, Informed Consent in Assessments; and 10.01, Informed Consent to Therapy.)

Essential Elements

Informed consent is an essential process that lays the foundation for all of a psychologist's professional activities regardless of role, setting, or medium used. Informed consent is a collaborative process that should be periodically revisited as a professional relationship evolves. Psychologists obtain informed consent before providing services and do so using language that is reasonably understandable; informed consent is designed to help others make informed, autonomous, and responsible decisions about participation in treatment (Standard 10.01), research (Standard 8.02), or educational programs (Standard 7). In those situations in which obtaining an individual's informed consent is not practical or required by law, psychologists engage in other actions to attempt to meet the obligations of this standard. Even in the case of court-ordered treatment, sufficient information must first be provided so that the individual understands the services to be provided and any limits to confidentiality that exist. All such efforts mandated in this standard must be documented and maintained in accordance with other standards for documentation and record keeping. Thorough informed consent is congruent with Principle E (Respect for People's Rights and Dignity) as well as the principle of autonomy.

Common Dilemmas and Conflicts

- Psychologists who fear that rigorous informed consent may reduce client disclosure may be less inclined to fulfill this obligation; research reveals no negative link between informed consent and disclosure or comfort in psychotherapy.
- It is often unclear whether a minor, his or her parent, or both should provide informed consent; psychologists who are unfamiliar with state laws bearing on age and consent to treatment may struggle in this area.
- Psychologists who fail to provide careful informed consent, who fail to document consent for participation, or who assume that informed consent occurs only once—at the outset of a relationship—are more inclined to have trouble in this area.

Prevention and Positive Practice

- ✓ All professional relationships (assessment, consulting, psychotherapy, research) should begin with informed consent, and it should be an ongoing process.
- ✓ Key elements of informed consent in counseling or psychotherapy include: the nature of services and expected treatment outcomes, its voluntary nature and the right to withdraw, available alternatives and their relative risks and benefits, fees, missed appointment and billing policies, insurance matters, limits to confidentiality, emergency contact procedures, use of consultation by the psychologist, and likelihood or risks of discomfort.
- ✓ Provide informed consent in both verbal and written formats and obtain participant signatures; take time to answer any questions, clarify concerns, and ensure their understanding.

✓ Always be familiar with relevant state or provincial laws bearing on age of consent and obligations to obtain parental consent; remember that requirements for consent may vary on the basis of the presenting problem, type of treatment, and the legal status of a minor.

✓ When evaluating an individual's capacity to give consent, be sure to explain all procedures and policies to the individual in a manner most likely to be understood by that person.

3.11 Psychological Services Delivered To or Through Organizations

(a) **Psychologists delivering services to or through organizations provide information beforehand to clients and when appropriate those directly affected by the services about (1) the nature and objectives of the services, (2) the intended recipients, (3) which of the individuals are clients, (4) the relationship the psychologist will have with each person and the organization, (5) the probable uses of services provided and information obtained, (6) who will have access to the information, and (7) limits of confidentiality. As soon as feasible, they provide information about the results and conclusions of such services to appropriate persons.**

(b) **If psychologists will be precluded by law or by organizational roles from providing such information to particular individuals or groups, they so inform those individuals or groups at the outset of the service.**

Essential Elements

At times, psychologists may provide services to or through organizations. Before doing so, all parties involved should first be informed about the nature of the services to be provided, who is likely to be involved and impacted, the identity of the primary client, who will have access to information from the services provided, and any limits to confidentiality that exist. Should anyone not have the right to any of this information, he or she should be informed of this fact prior to the services being provided.

Common Dilemmas and Conflicts

- Psychologists working for organizations may sometimes feel like "double agents"; they may be confused or conflicted about the identity of the primary client and whether their loyalty should be with individuals or the larger organization.
- At times, the best interests of an individual client and those of the organization may be incongruent.
- Psychologists who depend on organizations for their livelihood may feel greater pressure to fulfill obligations to their employer at the occasional expense of ethical obligations to individuals with whom they work.
- Psychologists who mistakenly assume that organizational demands may rival or even trump ethical obligations are at risk in this area.

Prevention and Positive Practice

- ✓ Before delivering any service in or through an organization, carefully inform stakeholders in the organization of your ethical obligations to each individual you engage professionally.
- ✓ Whether providing assessment, consultation, research, selection, treatment, or other services, provide thorough informed consent to all consumers of your work.
- ✓ In addition to key components of informed consent noted in Standard 3.10, clarify your role with all parties involved, your obligations to all parties, the manner in which any information about the person may be used, and limits to confidentiality.
- ✓ If a conflict emerges between the demands of the organization and your obligations under the Ethics Code, clearly explain your obligations under the Code and adhere to them carefully (see Standard 1.03).

3.12 Interruption of Psychological Services

Unless otherwise covered by contract, psychologists make reasonable efforts to plan for facilitating services in the event that psychological services are interrupted

by factors such as the psychologist's illness, death, un-availability, relocation, or retirement or by the client's/patient's relocation or financial limitations. (See also Standard 6.02c, Maintenance, Dissemination, and Disposal of Confidential Records of Professional and Scientific Work.)

Essential Elements

To prevent client abandonment and to best fulfill their obligation to meet their clients' ongoing treatment needs, psychologists make advance arrangements for emergency coverage and access to client records during periods of planned as well as unanticipated absence or unavailability. Psychologists are responsible for making reasonable efforts to ensure that their clients' needs are appropriately met when services are interrupted. Psychologists should have policies in place for responding to changes in clients' financial resources so that abandonment does not occur. Because clients at times continue their treatment with other professionals, policies that address the mechanisms for the transfer of clients' records should be in place. Thoughtful advanced planning is required to avoid harm to clients stemming from an interruption of services.

Common Dilemmas and Conflicts

- When a client is harmed by the interruption of psychological services—often as a result of poor preparation by a psychologist—there are few, if any, legitimate excuses.
- Psychologists who engage in denial regarding the potential for loss of employment, a failed practice, family emergencies, prolonged illness, disability, or even death, are more likely to be unprepared for these occurrences.
- Psychologists who are disorganized and fail to keep records up-to-date are more likely to create interruptions in services should they become incapacitated.
- Once a professional relationship has begun, if the client has ongoing treatment needs, a psychologist cannot simply cease service provision—no matter the reason—without working toward a smooth transition to an alternative service provider.

Prevention and Positive Practice

✓ Make advanced arrangements with a trusted colleague for coverage of your clients in the case of your illness or incapacity. Be certain that this colleague can obtain an updated list of client contact information and instructions for locating and accessing records.

✓ Make this arrangement clear to your clients during the informed consent process.

✓ Consult with an attorney to create a professional will that will ensure that your executor and family will collaborate with this colleague—licensed in your state—to expeditiously notify and provide for your clients.

✓ A professional will should address essential tasks including notifying clients, helping clients locate new providers, ensuring timely transfer of records, and the long-term maintenance, storage, and disposal of existing records.

✓ Keep all records up-to-date.

Standard 4. Privacy and Confidentiality

4.01 Maintaining Confidentiality

Psychologists have a primary obligation and take reasonable precautions to protect confidential information obtained through or stored in any medium, recognizing that the extent and limits of confidentiality may be regulated by law or established by institutional rules or professional or scientific relationship. (See also Standard 2.05, Delegation of Work to Others.)

Essential Elements

The protection of information shared by clients and others is a fundamental obligation of all psychologists and is also a legal mandate. Regardless of the nature of the professional relationship (e.g., psychotherapy, supervision, research, consultation) or the medium involved (e.g., written materials, audio- and videotapes, faxes, e-mail, phone messages), psychologists must take appropriate steps to ensure that confidentiality is not breeched inappropriately. At times regulations, laws, and institutional policies may impact these efforts so psychologists must always be aware of them and work to maximize the protection of confidential information.

Common Dilemmas and Conflicts

- Psychologists may erroneously assume that staff, supervisees, and subordinates understand and work to vigorously protect each individual's confidentiality.
- Laws, regulations, and organizational policies may conflict with the intent of the ethical mandate to maintain confidentiality and present challenges for psychologists working in these settings.
- Psychologists using various media may underestimate the threats to confidentiality related to new technologies and may fail to take necessary precautions.
- Psychologists must balance the requirement to create a thorough and reliable record (Standard 6.01) with the duty to safeguard the confidentiality of the material therein.

Prevention and Positive Practice

✓ Proactively consider all potential threats to confidentiality and take preventative steps prior to commencing any professional activity.

✓ Frequently remind yourself that confidentiality is central to any helping relationship and crucial to the public image of psychology.

✓ Carefully train all staff, supervisees, and subordinates in the steps necessary to protect each individual's confidentiality and periodically review and reinforce this training.

✓ Establish appropriate office policies bearing on the use of technology (e.g., faxes, e-mails, phone messages, client recordings) to prevent inadvertent disclosures of client material.

✓ When unsure of the best strategies to protect confidentiality, consult with an experienced colleague or ethics committee.

4.02 Discussing the Limits of Confidentiality

(a) **Psychologists discuss with persons (including, to the extent feasible, persons who are legally incapable of giving informed consent and their legal representatives) and organizations with whom they establish a scientific or professional relationship (1) the relevant limits of confidentiality and (2) the foreseeable uses**

of the information generated through their psychological activities. (See also Standard 3.10, Informed
Consent.)
(b) Unless it is not feasible or is contraindicated, the discussion of confidentiality occurs at the outset of the
relationship and thereafter as new circumstances
may warrant.
(c) Psychologists who offer services, products, or information via electronic transmission inform clients/
patients of the risks to privacy and limits of confidentiality.

Essential Elements

Confidentiality and its limits are essential issues to include in
every informed consent agreement and should occur at the outset of the professional relationship unless this is not possible,
such as in the case of emergency situations. This informed consent process occurs with all recipients of psychologists' services
whether individuals, groups, or organizations. Clients should
understand in advance any foreseeable instances in which case
material could be disclosed outside the professional relationship.
If individuals are not able or legally competent to fully participate in this process, relevant information is shared with their
legal representatives, and as much as is feasible, with those individuals as well. In addition to discussing all reasonably likely limits to confidentiality, the potential uses of information shared
should be reviewed as well. When any technologies are used that
may impact confidentiality, the psychologist first shares information about the risks of using these media so that the individual
may make a fully informed decision about their use.

Common Dilemmas and Conflicts

- It may be tempting to assume that all clients understand
  and appreciate the limits of confidentiality, but doing so
  may increase the probability of violating clients' rights.
- Psychologists who assume that a single discussion about
  confidentiality at the outset of the professional relationship is adequate may fail to anticipate and process new
  threats to confidentiality as they arise.

■ Those using various technologies to provide services, to store records, or to communicate with clients may be unaware of the significant risks to confidentiality that these technologies generate.

Prevention and Positive Practice

✓ Discuss all potential limits to confidentiality with each client from the outset as part of the informed consent process.

✓ Even when an individual is incapable of giving informed consent, attempt to convey this information at a level he or she can comprehend. Additionally, this information should be shared with the individual's legal representative.

✓ Discuss the limits of confidentiality openly and thoroughly at the beginning of the professional relationship and then continually update this dimension of informed consent as new risks, threats, or requirements impacting confidentiality arise.

✓ When using various technologies, consider their limitations and share this information with clients in advance so they understand all potential limits to confidentiality.

4.03 Recording

Before recording the voices or images of individuals to whom they provide services, psychologists obtain permission from all such persons or their legal representatives. (See also Standards 8.03, Informed Consent for Recording Voices and Images in Research; 8.05, Dispensing With Informed Consent for Research; and 8.07, Deception in Research.)

Essential Elements

It is often appropriate and helpful to use audio- or videotape recording with clients such as during training or when receiving supervision. Psychologists should carefully explain the rationale for recording any part of their work with others, including the disposition of recordings after they are created. Psychologists should also take time to process any reservations on the part of those involved and honor any person's refusal. Before using any recording equipment, psychologists must first obtain informed consent from each client, group member, student, or research participant involved. When a child or other person unable to provide appropriate consent is involved, psychologists secure informed consent from the appropriate guardian before proceeding.

Common Dilemmas and Conflicts

- Psychologists functioning in training settings may erroneously assume that clients expect recording to occur for training purposes and therefore that their specific consent is not needed.
- Those using recordings for their own personal purposes with no intention of sharing them with others may erroneously assume that consent is not needed from the individual client, student, or research subject.
- With minors or others not competent to give consent, psychologists may erroneously assume that merely explaining the recording to them without obtaining informed consent from their legal representative is adequate.
- Psychologists sometimes forget that all recordings of clients must be carefully maintained, protected, and properly disposed of.

Prevention and Positive Practice

✓ Never audio- or videotape any individual without first receiving his or her explicit written consent to do so.

✓ Avoid assuming that a client, student, or subject shares your expectations or understanding regarding the use of recording devices.

✓ Remember that clients' specific consent is required before they may be recorded, even if recordings will not be shared with others.

✓ If a client is unable to give competent informed consent, make an effort to explain the purpose of the recording, seek the client's approval, and then obtain consent from the legal representative before any recording occurs.

4.04 Minimizing Intrusions on Privacy

(a) **Psychologists include in written and oral reports and consultations, only information germane to the purpose for which the communication is made.**

(b) **Psychologists discuss confidential information obtained in their work only for appropriate scientific or professional purposes and only with persons clearly concerned with such matters.**

Essential Elements

Psychologists take special care to protect each client's confidentiality in written reports, verbal presentations, and consultations. Only information relevant to the agreed-on purpose of the report, presentation, or consultation should be included. When clients consent to releasing confidential information, psychologists are careful not to exceed the breadth of their consent by sharing additional confidential information not included in the disclosure agreement. Further, this implies that confidential information is being shared for appropriate professional purposes and with appropriate authorization. Confidential information should never be shared with others outside of a professional context. Only those individuals with a legitimate professional need to have access to confidential information should be allowed to obtain it.

Common Dilemmas and Conflicts

- It may at times be tempting to share more information about a client or student than is required or authorized.
- It may be very challenging not to share confidential information with family and friends, especially if working with difficult or high-profile clients or when under stress.
- In high stress situations—such as when making a mandatory child abuse report—there is greater risk of sharing information that goes beyond that which is relevant to filing the report.

Prevention and Positive Practice

✓ Remain cognizant of the specific limits set for sharing confidential information in written and verbal reports and consultations.
✓ Only information directly relevant to a referral question, consultation, or evaluation should be included in your appropriate disclosures or records.

✓ Remind yourself that privacy is a fundamental right; even when another professional or entity has received appropriate informed consent, only material directly germane to the reason for disclosure should be offered.

4.05 Disclosures

(a) Psychologists may disclose confidential information with the appropriate consent of the organizational client, the individual client/patient, or another legally authorized person on behalf of the client/patient unless prohibited by law.

(b) Psychologists disclose confidential information without the consent of the individual only as mandated by law, or where permitted by law for a valid purpose such as to (1) provide needed professional services; (2) obtain appropriate professional consultations; (3) protect the client/patient, psychologist, or others from harm; or (4) obtain payment for services from a client/patient, in which instance disclosure is limited to the minimum that is necessary to achieve the purpose. (See also Standard 6.04e, Fees and Financial Arrangements.)

Essential Elements

When a client or other person entitled to confidentiality provides appropriate informed consent, a psychologist may disclose otherwise protected information about the person. In more unusual circumstances, a psychologist may disclose confidential information without the consent of the person entitled to confidentiality. Some of the most common reasons for such unauthorized disclosures include the following: (a) The client is at significant risk of causing harm to self or others; (b) there is evidence of child or elder abuse; (c) a legitimate court orders release of information; (d) the client files a complaint or initiates litigation against the psychologist; (e) the client is involved in other litigation and has introduced his or her relationship with the psychologist into evidence; (f) the client is so impaired that involuntary treatment is indicated under state law; or (g) state or federal laws mandate disclosure for other purposes. Because laws and statutes bearing on such disclosures vary across time and jurisdiction, psychologists must remain up-to-date with regard to local legislation. Even when a disclosure is approved by the client or required by law, the psychologist should be cautious to avoid unnecessary violations of privacy.

Common Dilemmas and Conflicts

- Psychologists who fail to remain current and cognizant of state and federal laws bearing on disclosures of confidential material are at greater risk in this area.
- At times, disclosures allowed by the Ethics Code may be prohibited by state law, or disclosures mandated by law may appear to violate the spirit of the Ethics Code. Psychologists must resolve these dilemmas with due regard for the client's best interest and respect for the law (see Standard 1.02).
- When a psychologist's decision threshold for making unauthorized disclosures is too low, he or she runs the risk of violating client confidentiality and Standard 4.01.

Prevention and Positive Practice

- ✓ Frequently review state and federal laws bearing on mandated disclosures of confidential information.
- ✓ Make discussions of the various reasons for disclosure part of the ongoing informed consent process.
- ✓ Remember that legal requirements for disclosure do not absolve you of the duty to maintain test security (Standard 9.11); never release copyrighted test items or materials without reviewing your contractual and legal obligations to the publisher.
- ✓ Never use a threat of disclosure to elicit payment from a client.
- ✓ When disclosure is required—either because it is authorized by the client or required by law—protect privacy (Standard 4.04) by disclosing only the information required.
- ✓ When questions arise regarding the need for an unauthorized disclosure, seek consultation from a colleague experienced in this area.
- ✓ Ensure familiarity with specific child- and elder-abuse-reporting laws in your jurisdiction.

4.06 Consultations

When consulting with colleagues, (1) psychologists do not disclose confidential information that reasonably could lead to the identification of a client/patient, research participant, or other person or organization with whom they have a confidential relationship unless they have obtained the prior consent of the person or organization or the disclosure cannot be avoided, and (2) they disclose information only to the extent necessary to achieve the purposes of the consultation. (See also Standard 4.01, Maintaining Confidentiality.)

Essential Elements

Making good use of professional consultations is an important part of ensuring competent practice (Standard 2) and an essential component of professional excellence. But psychologists must approach collegial consultation with due regard for the client's, student's, or research participant's right to privacy and confidentiality. When seeking consultation on a case, it is incumbent on the psychologist to disguise or eliminate those elements of the case or details about the person—whenever this is possible—that could lead to their being identified, unless the client consents to disclosure for the purpose of consultation. Finally, psychologists using collegial consultation should be careful to reveal only that information required to achieve the purposes of the consultation; they should be conservative when discussing their clients.

Common Dilemmas and Conflicts

- Psychologists who are careless about those they consult with, details about the client, or the context in which they consult are at risk in this area.
- When the desire to reveal particularly distressing, humorous, or shocking material about a client is strong, psychologists may run the risk of gossiping versus seeking genuine consultation.
- Psychologists who eschew consultation because of fear of being revealed as incompetent or who fear inadvertent disclosure of sensitive client information may diminish the quality of their services.

Prevention and Positive Practice

✓ Establish reciprocal consultation relationships with competent and experienced colleagues.

✓ Choose these colleagues carefully, and communicate expectations that all consultations will remain confidential.

✓ Whenever necessary, carefully eliminate or disguise material such that your client, research participant, student, or other person cannot reasonably be identified unless specific consent for the consultation and sharing identifying information is first received.

✓ Before disclosing client material in any consultation, ask the following questions:

- How will this consultation directly benefit the client?
- How would the client feel about this disclosure if he or she became aware of it?
- Is any part of this consultation for my own gratification?
- Is this colleague reliable and is the environment secure and professional?
- Did I discuss consultation as a potential limit to confidentiality?

✓ Provide clients with clear informed consent about ongoing consultation relationships.

4.07 Use of Confidential Information for Didactic or Other Purposes

> **Psychologists do not disclose in their writings, lectures, or other public media, confidential, personally identifiable information concerning their clients/patients, students, research participants, organizational clients, or other recipients of their services that they obtained during the course of their work, unless (1) they take reasonable steps to disguise the person or organization, (2) the person or organization has consented in writing, or (3) there is legal authorization for doing so.**

Essential Elements

When teaching, writing, or interacting with the media, it is often quite tempting to use material from a professional relationship to illustrate a concept or underscore a point. Yet, psychologists must avoid such illustrative disclosures unless the individuals or their legal representatives have given explicit consent for such disclosures, or psychologists have taken great care to either eliminate or disguise any detail about the person or their story that might lead to recognition or identification by others. Of course, this latter strategy always leaves some risk—even if remote—that confidential material will be linked to a client, student, or research subject. Psychologists must fully understand that the onus of responsibility for protecting the identity of their clients rests with them. Even when media coverage or public documents have already revealed a person's disorder, treatment, or other information, this person's psychologist remains bound by the duties to protect privacy and maintain confidentiality.

Common Dilemmas and Conflicts

- Psychologists who offer examples from their professional work impulsively and without careful consideration are more likely to inadvertently violate a person's confidentiality in public.
- Psychologists who use case examples to entertain rather than to carefully illustrate concepts, syndromes, or techniques may be less inclined to carefully screen material before it is used didactically.
- Merely changing the person's name and a few demographic details will often be inadequate measures for protecting a person's identity.
- Psychologists may erroneously assume that because client information has entered the public domain (e.g., media, the court system) they are free to use the material in presentations and publications.

Prevention and Positive Practice

- ✓ If detailed information about a client's experiences, presentation, or response to treatment is likely to be useful and instructive for teaching or other purposes, seek consent from the client for use of the material for didactic purposes and specify how the material will be used.
- ✓ If obtaining direct consent is not feasible or appropriate, it may be wise not to use the example or, if used, to disguise

enough of the facts and details that not even the person's close friends or relatives would recognize him or her in your presentation.

✓ Always test your illustrative client examples on an experienced colleague to be sure that you have not neglected to sanitize or alter any salient detail.

✓ In your writing and speaking, it is nearly always preferable to use amalgams of several cases to illustrate points so that no single individual could ever be linked with your examples.

Standard 5. Advertising and Other Public Statements

5.01 Avoidance of False or Deceptive Statements

(a) Public statements include but are not limited to paid or unpaid advertising, product endorsements, grant applications, licensing applications, other credentialing applications, brochures, printed matter, directory listings, personal resumes or curricula vitae, or comments for use in media such as print or electronic transmission, statements in legal proceedings, lectures and public oral presentations, and published materials. Psychologists do not knowingly make public statements that are false, deceptive, or fraudulent concerning their research, practice, or other work activities or those of persons or organizations with which they are affiliated.

(b) Psychologists do not make false, deceptive, or fraudulent statements concerning (1) their training, experience, or competence; (2) their academic degrees; (3) their credentials; (4) their institutional or association affiliations; (5) their services; (6) the scientific or clinical basis for, or results or degree of success of, their services; (7) their fees; or (8) their publications or research findings.

(c) Psychologists claim degrees as credentials for their health services only if those degrees (1) were earned from a regionally accredited educational institution

or (2) were the basis for psychology licensure by the state in which they practice.

Essential Elements

Psychologists make a wide range of public statements in the course of their professional activities. These may include advertisements, listings, resumes, workshops and lectures, publications, and presentations to the media. In all these and related public statements, psychologists must only include truthful and accurate information. Any misrepresentation of one's credentials, affiliations, experience, and the like, even if not overt falsehoods, must be avoided. Research findings must be presented clearly and accurately and psychologists must avoid misleading statistics or implications. Only those degrees and credentials that are earned from an accredited program—a program that could lead to licensure as a psychologist—may be included in statements to the public. Misrepresentation of any of these, be it explicit or implied, is considered exploitative and violates the public's trust in the profession.

Common Dilemmas and Conflicts

- In an effort to aggressively market their services, psychologists may be tempted to overstate their training, credentials, or the nature of their services to entice potential clients.
- Researchers may feel pressure to report findings that confirm their hypotheses and that increase the likelihood of additional funding, promotion, or tenure.
- Psychologists in the public eye who share their expertise with the media may be tempted to bolster their credibility by overstating credentials, experience, or the results of their work.
- Those being interviewed by the media may be pushed to make statements that go beyond available data, to share confidential information, or to provide treatment recommendations outside of a defined professional relationship.

Prevention and Positive Practice

✓ Present all degrees, training, credentials, and experience accurately and fully. Respect the lure of aggrandizement and adulation, and refuse to overstate or misstate credentials to the public.

✓ As clinicians, researchers, teachers, media presenters, and in all other roles, be sure all material is factually correct and that false impressions are not likely either through overt misrepresentations of fact or through implication.

✓ Present research findings accurately and honestly without allowing other pressures or motivations to adversely impact your truthfulness and integrity.

✓ Understand the obligation to be transparent not just to your clients but to all consumers of your services and work products.

✓ Have a trusted colleague review your professional material before publishing, posting, or otherwise disseminating it.

5.02 Statements by Others

(a) **Psychologists who engage others to create or place public statements that promote their professional practice, products, or activities retain professional responsibility for such statements.**

(b) **Psychologists do not compensate employees of press, radio, television, or other communication media in return for publicity in a news item. (See also Standard 1.01, Misuse of Psychologists' Work.)**

(c) **A paid advertisement relating to psychologists' activities must be identified or clearly recognizable as such.**

Essential Elements

Even when they hire others to assist with advertising, marketing, the development of brochures, and the like, psychologists maintain responsibility for the content of these materials and ensure that they are factually accurate. Psychologists must take reasonable steps to ensure their accuracy to avoid misrepresenting themselves to the public. Thus, they must provide effective oversight of those they employ for these activities. When they provide interviews or otherwise appear in the news media, they may never pay for this exposure. When advertising their services, unless it is explicitly clear that the public statement is an advertisement, all such activities must be clearly labeled as advertisements. It is essential that psychologists avoid presenting paid advertisements as something else, such as a public service announcement or scientific report.

Common Dilemmas and Conflicts

- When using the services of others for advertising, it may be tempting to assume that they both know and abide by the ethics standards of the profession of psychology.
- Those interested in marketing their practice may see opportunities for increased media exposure by compensating media employees for inclusion in news stories.
- Creative marketing in the media such as through infomercials and other on air activities may have the appearance of public service programming or educational programming.

Prevention and Positive Practice

- ✓ Closely monitor and supervise all employees and paid consultants who develop or disseminate public statements on your behalf to ensure that no misrepresentation or deception occurs.
- ✓ Never pay someone in the media to include you in a news item.
- ✓ Be sure all advertising activities are clearly labeled as such and that all advertising is truthful and not deceptive.
- ✓ Always request predissemination review of any material promoting your services or work; require the right of final approval.

5.03 Descriptions of Workshops and Non-Degree-Granting Educational Programs

To the degree to which they exercise control, psychologists responsible for announcements, catalogs, brochures, or advertisements describing workshops, seminars, or other non-degree-granting educational programs ensure that they accurately describe the audience for which the program is intended, the educational objectives, the presenters, and the fees involved.

Essential Elements

Psychologists may provide presentations such as workshops, seminars, community talks, and other educational programs. They must make a reasonable effort to ensure that all advertisements, marketing materials, brochures, and the like are accurate with regard to content, the appropriate audience, educational objectives, presenters and credentials, and any fees involved. They should always carefully review the content of all such materials before they are disseminated to the public to ensure that no misrepresentation occurs. They must avoid assuming that others will take this responsibility for them.

Common Dilemmas and Conflicts

- It may be tempting to assume that individuals who prepare brochures and other marketing materials for psychologists will ensure their accuracy.
- Psychologists offering seminars and workshops may erroneously assume that standards bearing on descriptions may be less rigorous than those common in academic settings.
- Psychologists who typically provide clinical services may assume that protections and safeguards are not needed when developing promotional materials for presentations.

Prevention and Positive Practice

- ✓ Always be sure to provide accurate information in all materials that describe presentations.
- ✓ Insist that presenters provide current and accurate information about their credentials and that presentations adhere to the published objectives and content.
- ✓ When responsible for any educational program or workshop, insist on the right to give final approval before promotional or educational material is disseminated.
- ✓ Always include adequate information in these materials so the public can make a fully informed decision about participation.

5.04 Media Presentations

When psychologists provide public advice or comment via print, Internet, or other electronic transmission, they take precautions to ensure that statements (1) are based on their professional knowledge, training, or experience in accord with appropriate psychological literature and practice; (2) are otherwise consistent with this Ethics Code; and (3) do not indicate that a professional relationship has been established with the recipient. (See also Standard 2.04, Bases for Scientific and Professional Judgments.)

Essential Elements

When psychologists offer advice or make presentations to the public through print, Internet, or electronic media outlets, they stand to offer a great service to the public while enhancing the public image of psychology. On the downside, the glamour and flattery associated with an invitation to make a media presentation may overshadow good judgment and professionalism. When asked to give an interview or make a media presentation, psychologists must be sure that their comments are valid, based on legitimate evidence, consistent with the Ethics Code, and likely to further public confidence in the profession. Psychologists must be particularly vigilant to avoid the impression that a professional relationship has been established with those they interact with during presentations; dispensing professional advice to individuals is generally not recommended.

Common Dilemmas and Conflicts

- Psychologists may sacrifice prudence and caution during media presentations to make an impression or please a journalist.
- During the course of a media presentation, it may be tempting to respond to queries that clearly range outside the boundaries of one's demonstrated competence.
- Psychologists who are eager to make an impression or promote themselves may also be inclined to overstate the evidence supporting their comments.
- Psychologists who fail to insist on some control of the presentation and the way in which their public comments will be presented may be at greater risk of misrepresentation.

Prevention and Positive Practice

✓ Unless you are experienced in doing so, avoid spontaneous comments to media outlets; before making any public comment, carefully consider the nature of the request, the "agenda" of the journalist, and your own competence in the area.

✓ Be assertive about the ground rules for interviews and presentations; exert some control over the format and ask to review a print copy before your comments are published.

✓ Carefully consider the scientific and experiential basis for your comments. How would a jury of your peers evaluate the veracity of your claims?

✓ Thoughtfully consider the potential impact of your comments on the public and on the broader profession of psychology.

✓ Refuse to participate in any media interaction when you believe there is a reasonable chance that your comments will be misused or when it is clear that the outlet has a reputation for sensational or distorted reporting.

✓ Avoid dispensing professional advice directly to individuals during public presentations.

5.05 Testimonials

Psychologists do not solicit testimonials from current therapy clients/patients or other persons who because of their particular circumstances are vulnerable to undue influence.

Essential Elements

Psychologists hold positions of power and trust in relation to those they serve. Psychologists must not ask current therapy clients to offer testimonials or endorsements of their services because such solicitation raises the possibility of exploitation or self-serving influence on the part of the psychologist. Psychologists must neither solicit nor accept offers for testimonials from current clients. It is also recommended that psychologists avoid using testimonials from former clients because they may still be dependent on the psychologist's view of them and may return in the future for further treatment.

Common Dilemmas and Conflicts

- Psychologists who minimize the power differential between themselves and their clients and psychologists who fail to understand the dangers of conflict-of-interest situations may be at greater risk in this area.
- Both current and former clients are vulnerable to undue influence by a psychologist.
- As a result of transference and power differences between psychologists and clients, it is doubtful that any current client's testimonial would be truly objective and unbiased.
- Focusing on psychologists' own needs over their clients' needs places them at risk for impaired judgment and decision making.

Prevention and Positive Practice

- ✓ Never solicit and, if offered by a current therapy client, politely refuse any testimonial regarding your services.
- ✓ Never assume that clients can freely give their consent to such a request; their offer may reflect a wish to please you but may not be in their best interests.
- ✓ Remember that any public testimonial on the part of current or former therapy clients may raise concerns about exploitation.

5.06 In-Person Solicitation

Psychologists do not engage, directly or through agents, in uninvited in-person solicitation of business from actual or potential therapy clients/patients or other persons who because of their particular circumstances are vulnerable to undue influence. However, this prohibition does not preclude (1) attempting to implement appropriate collateral contacts for the purpose of benefiting an already engaged therapy client/patient or (2) providing disaster or community outreach services.

Essential Elements

Psychologists should never engage in direct solicitation of business from either current therapy clients or potential clients. Such solicitation is seen as both unprofessional and intrusive; it has the potential to be exploitive and manipulative—especially when those solicited are vulnerable. Psychologists are accorded deference as holders of knowledge and expertise, and others are naturally vulnerable to any suggestion that psychologists' services may be necessary. Of course, it is perfectly ethical to offer services free of charge as part of community outreach or other pro bono service, and it is appropriate, with a client's consent, to involve other persons in a client's treatment as long as this is purely in the client's interest and not a strategy on the part of the psychologist for soliciting new clients.

Common Dilemmas and Conflicts

- New psychologists or those in tenuous financial situations may be tempted to directly solicit business.
- Even when psychologists believe others will likely benefit from their services, in-person solicitation may violate privacy, may feel exploitive, and may diminish the public image of psychology.

Prevention and Positive Practice

✓ Never directly solicit business from current therapy clients, and make sure that business partners, supervisees, and employees also avoid such activity.

✓ Remember that those most likely to require psychological services are also most likely to be vulnerable to the influence of psychologists' "expert" suggestions.

✓ Be especially cautious to avoid appealing to any person's fear regarding the risks associated with not seeking your services.

✓ When offering pro bono, disaster relief, community outreach, or collateral services for a client, carefully avoid any impression that you are seeking to solicit new clients.

Standard 6. Record Keeping and Fees

6.01 Documentation of Professional and Scientific Work and Maintenance of Records

Psychologists create, and to the extent the records are under their control, maintain, disseminate, store, retain, and dispose of records and data relating to their professional and scientific work in order to (1) facilitate provision of services later by them or by other professionals, (2) allow for replication of research design and analyses, (3) meet institutional requirements, (4) ensure accuracy of billing and payments, and (5) ensure compliance with law. (See also Standard 4.01, Maintaining Confidentiality.)

Essential Elements

This standard makes the documentation of all services provided by psychologists an ethical mandate. It also highlights several of the reasons for documenting the services they provide. These rationales should prove useful to guide psychologists when deciding on the exact content, specificity, and format of documentation. Additionally, psychologists are directed to maintain, store, retain, and dispose of records and data in accordance with the Ethics Code (e.g., maintaining confidentiality) to the extent that records are under their control. For example, those working in hospital settings or government agencies may not have full control over the records they create, and the records department of the institution may carry the primary responsibility for managing and protecting records. But, to the extent possible, psychologists should ensure that their clients,' students,' supervisees,' and research subjects' right to confidentiality is not violated and that clients maintain appropriate access to their records. Finally, this standard requires psychologists to be accurate in records of their billing and payments.

Common Dilemmas and Conflicts

- Psychologists working in a group practice or organizational setting may be tempted to assume that others will ensure that the requirements of this standard are met.
- Attention to the American Psychological Association (APA) Ethics Code is important but to overlook relevant state laws will place the psychologist at risk as well.
- Psychologists attempting to reduce malpractice risk by keeping minimal documentation of services provided will inadvertently increase their risk by violating this standard and possibly state law as well.

Prevention and Positive Practice

- ✓ Carefully document your work and ensure that all documentation is accurate.
- ✓ Abide by relevant state laws regarding the composition of records, how they are retained and stored, and how and when they may be destroyed.
- ✓ Store and dispose of records thoughtfully and with assurance that confidentiality is not violated.
- ✓ When working in group or organizational settings, ensure that others with responsibility over records are aware of and follow both the APA Ethics Code and relevant state laws.
- ✓ Remember that the documentation of your work may be used for a variety of appropriate purposes; excellent records create enough detail, specificity, and accuracy to facilitate provision of services later.

6.02 Maintenance, Dissemination, and Disposal of Confidential Records of Professional and Scientific Work

(a) Psychologists maintain confidentiality in creating, storing, accessing, transferring, and disposing of records under their control, whether these are written, automated, or in any other medium. (See also Standards 4.01, Maintaining Confidentiality, and 6.01, Documentation of Professional and Scientific Work and Maintenance of Records.)

(b) If confidential information concerning recipients of psychological services is entered into databases or systems of records available to persons whose access has not been consented to by the recipient, psychologists use coding or other techniques to avoid the inclusion of personal identifiers.

(c) Psychologists make plans in advance to facilitate the appropriate transfer and to protect the confidentiality of records and data in the event of psychologists' withdrawal from positions or practice. (See also Standards 3.12, Interruption of Psychological Services, and 10.09, Interruption of Therapy.)

Essential Elements

Precautions must be taken in the creation, storage, transfer, and disposal of all records to ensure their confidentiality regardless of the medium used. Psychologists should anticipate potential threats to privacy such as who may have access to record storage facilities or computer systems and take appropriate precautions to prevent breaches of security. For example, all written records should be stored under lock and key, and all electronic records should be password protected. When confidential information is included in databases, this requires special care. If the information can be accessed by individuals for whom the recipient of services has not consented, identifying information should first be removed so that each individual's identity may be protected. Psychologists should always make arrangements in advance to ensure that the confidentiality of records is maintained even if they are no longer present at the location or in the organization in which services were provided. This should be addressed clearly in employment contracts or through the use of a professional will (see Standard 3.12).

Common Dilemmas and Conflicts

- Psychologists using a range of media for the documentation and storage of their work face a range of threats to the privacy and confidentiality of those they serve.
- Assuming that others will not have access to records or that those who do have access will follow the APA Ethics Code and state laws may lead to lax practices that result in unintended breaches of privacy.
- Failure to address and clarify the responsibility for protecting records' security in advance may result in unintended breaches should the psychologist leave a position.
- Researchers may view this standard as more relevant to clinical records and fail to appropriately address the preservation of research data's confidentiality.

Prevention and Positive Practice

- ✓ Create and follow clear policies for all data and records to ensure that breaches of confidentiality do not occur.
- ✓ Use various technologies (computers, faxes, etc.) with great care and attention to threats to confidentiality.
- ✓ Use security measures to prevent unauthorized access to confidential records and data.
- ✓ Use a written agreement that specifies responsibilities and steps to be taken to maintain and preserve the confidentiality of all records and data should you leave your position or practice.
- ✓ It is particularly important to follow the Health Insurance Portability and Accountability Act (HIPAA) Security Rule in this area.

6.03 Withholding Records for Nonpayment

Psychologists may not withhold records under their control that are requested and needed for a client's/patient's

emergency treatment solely because payment has not been received.

Essential Elements

Psychologists rightly expect payment for all professional services provided, and this issue should always be addressed clearly in the informed consent process at the outset of the professional relationship. But, at times, clients may fall behind in their financial obligations, either unintentionally as a result of financial hardship or possibly even intentionally. Regardless of the reason for nonpayment, or psychologists' feelings about it, psychologists must balance their right to be compensated with each client's clinical needs. Should a client make a formal request for his or her records for emergency treatment (as opposed to just wanting a copy for his or her personal records), psychologists must provide these records regardless of fees owed.

Common Dilemmas and Conflicts

- Psychologists may become angry or resentful when clients owe money for services rendered and do not make promised payments. Such emotional reactions may cloud psychologists' judgment.
- Clients' stated reasons for failure to make required payments may easily impact psychologists' decisions regarding requests for records for emergency treatment.
- Determining just what constitutes emergency treatment requires a consideration of the facts of the particular situation and the application of reasonable professional judgment.

Prevention and Positive Practice

- ✓ Fully address issues of nonpayment in the informed consent process and make an effort to prevent accumulation of a significant balance.
- ✓ Respond to requests for records in a timely manner and make the client's clinical needs your primary consideration.
- ✓ When deciding what constitutes an emergency situation, always err in favor of meeting clients' clinical needs.

✓ Consider implications of the HIPAA Privacy Rule when applying this standard.

6.04 Fees and Financial Arrangements

(a) As early as is feasible in a professional or scientific relationship, psychologists and recipients of psychological services reach an agreement specifying compensation and billing arrangements.

(b) Psychologists' fee practices are consistent with law.

(c) Psychologists do not misrepresent their fees.

(d) If limitations to services can be anticipated because of limitations in financing, this is discussed with the recipient of services as early as is feasible. (See also Standards 10.09, Interruption of Therapy, and 10.10, Terminating Therapy.)

(e) If the recipient of services does not pay for services as agreed, and if psychologists intend to use collection agencies or legal measures to collect the fees, psychologists first inform the person that such measures will be taken and provide that person an opportunity to make prompt payment. (See also Standards 4.05, Disclosures; 6.03, Withholding Records for Nonpayment; and 10.01, Informed Consent to Therapy.)

Essential Elements

Conflicts and misunderstandings related to fees and financial arrangements constitute one of the most frequent and preventable sources of ethical and legal complaints against psychologists. Psychologists must be proactive by being both thorough and transparent in discussing all financial arrangements with clients at the outset of any professional relationship. Discussions of fees and financial arrangements should be part of the ongoing informed consent process with clients. Psychologists must ensure that their fee practices are consistent with relevant state and federal laws, that all fee practices are accurately represented up front, and that if a collection agency is employed in certain circumstances, clients are clearly informed about this practice and the circumstances in which it would apply as early as possible in treatment. Psychologists should also demonstrate sensitivity to a client's financial circumstances at the outset of any relationship and work to both anticipate and avoid interruption in a client's treatment or premature treatment termination based on financial constraints. In all financial matters, psychologists are fair, transparent, and inclined to carefully attend to their clients' best interests.

Common Dilemmas and Conflicts

- It is easy to erroneously assume that clients will read and understand fee practices included in an informed consent document.
- Psychologists may unnecessarily escalate conflict over fees or an unpaid balance by failing to be flexible and work with clients before turning to a collection agency.
- Psychologists who fail to recognize that clients are often vulnerable to financial exploitation and who fail to act in clients' best interests in this regard are at risk in this area.
- Psychologists who engage collection agency services without careful informed consent, without goodwill efforts to resolve the financial problem informally, and without careful scrutiny of the agency's practices may find themselves at odds with state laws and the Ethics Code.

Prevention and Positive Practice

- ✓ At the beginning of any professional relationship, and as often as indicated thereafter, work to ensure that clients understand all of your fees and financial practices (e.g., charges for various services, amount covered by insurance, when payment is expected, consequences of nonpayment).
- ✓ Consider a client's financial situation—including relevant insurance—at the outset of treatment and avoid terminating services abruptly when insurance coverage expires.
- ✓ If the length of indicated treatment far exceeds a client's ability to pay, consider a reduced fee, pro bono service, or a referral to a professional better able to meet the client's clinical needs under these financial circumstances.
- ✓ Be cautious about raising fees with existing clients; offer considerable notice before doing so; and consider the possible impact on their ability to continue treatment with a higher fee.

✓ Never charge different fees to clients based exclusively on variables unrelated to financial circumstances (e.g., race, gender, religion).

✓ Inform clients of the maximum outstanding balance you will allow and address nonpayment proactively as it occurs.

✓ Before engaging a collection agency,

  ▪ be certain a client has had clear informed consent about this practice;

  ▪ make reasonable efforts to collect the payment informally;

  ▪ inform the client before moving forward with collection;

  ▪ carefully consider the clinical implications of this action; and

  ▪ consider your own attitude (e.g., hostility) and level of flexibility.

✓ Remember that you are responsible for the behavior of any collection agency acting on your behalf; be especially vigilant about preventing violations of confidentiality when using such an agency.

✓ Never share clinical information with a collection agency, only name, date of service, and fees owed.

✓ Demonstrate attention to your clients' best interests. At times, the wisest course of action—and the course least likely to result in an ethics complaint—will involve writing off an unpaid balance; remind yourself to consider the big picture!

6.05 Barter With Clients/Patients

Barter is the acceptance of goods, services, or other non-monetary remuneration from clients/patients in return for psychological services. Psychologists may barter only if (1) it is not clinically contraindicated, and (2) the resulting arrangement is not exploitative. (See also Standards 3.05, Multiple Relationships, and 6.04, Fees and Financial Arrangements.)

Essential Elements

As a general rule, it is unwise to barter with clients. Accepting goods, services, or other nonmonetary compensation for professional services opens the door to misunderstandings, perceived or actual exploitation, boundary violations, and diminished efficacy in one's professional role. At the same time, agreeing to a bartering arrangement can be a humanitarian, culturally sensitive, and clinically indicated decision—particularly when a client's financial circumstances would otherwise prevent access to services. A decision to accept a bartering exchange with a client should follow careful determination that this best serves the client's interests and that the client is comfortable with the terms of the exchange. Before engaging in such an arrangement, psychologists should seek consultation from a trusted colleague who can objectively evaluate the proposed arrangement in terms of apparent equity, clinical contraindications, potential for exploitation (Standard 3.08), and the danger of potentially harmful multiple relationships (Standard 3.05).

Common Dilemmas and Conflicts

- It is often difficult to ensure that a bartering arrangement will be equitable to each party and difficult to predict whether the client will later feel disadvantaged or exploited by the arrangement.
- Psychologists who assume that clients can make objective and self-promoting decisions about bartering exchanges may be more likely to exploit clients.
- Psychologists who ignore the clinical and transference/countertransference implications of bartering may undermine the value of the services they provide.
- Psychologists should remember that bartering for services entails greater risk of misunderstanding and friction than bartering for goods, especially if the goods have a preestablished value.

Prevention and Positive Practice

- ✓ Whenever possible, avoid bartering arrangements with those you serve.
- ✓ When bartering is indicated to ensure that a client has access to services (i.e., when it is clearly in the client's best interest), proceed with caution.
- ✓ Reach an agreement on the value of each good or service in advance and consult with colleagues to be sure this is done fairly so that clients are not exploited.

✓ Carefully consider and discuss the clinical implications of this arrangement with clients.

✓ Revisit discussions of the bartering arrangement with a client throughout the course of treatment to ensure that the arrangement remains appropriate and satisfactory to the client.

6.06 Accuracy in Reports to Payors and Funding Sources

In their reports to payors for services or sources of research funding, psychologists take reasonable steps to ensure the accurate reporting of the nature of the service provided or research conducted, the fees, charges, or payments, and where applicable, the identity of the provider, the findings, and the diagnosis. (See also Standards 4.01, Maintaining Confidentiality; 4.04, Minimizing Intrusions on Privacy; and 4.05, Disclosures.)

Essential Elements

Psychologists are ethically obligated to be thoroughly accurate, precise, and transparent when reporting the nature of their services. This means that psychologists are careful to avoid any misrepresentation of a client's condition or diagnosis, assessments administered, indicated treatments, services actually rendered, research conducted, clinical or research outcomes, and the specific details concerning all services provided (e.g., dates, times, specific identity of provider, type of service). Psychologists must recognize that intentional misrepresentation of services to payors or funding sources constitutes fraud, which may have both legal and ethical repercussions. Finally, psychologists balance requirements for accuracy and transparency in reporting services rendered with other ethical obligations such as the maintenance of confidentiality (Standard 4.01), minimizing intrusions on privacy (Standard 4.04), and disclosures of client information (Standard 4.05).

Common Dilemmas and Conflicts

■ Psychologists who are struggling financially may be tempted to generate additional income from payors or funding sources by bending the truth and inaccurately reporting the nature and extent of services rendered.

■ Because insurance companies or other payors may not cover all the services provided by a psychologist, it may be very tempting to misrepresent the diagnosis, type of treatment, or other facts about services rendered.

■ Psychologists who convince themselves that misrepresentation of a client's condition or treatment is actually in the client's best interest —financially or clinically—are at considerable risk in this area.

Prevention and Positive Practice

✓ Be clear in your informed consent process that you will be thoroughly accurate in your reporting of all assessment and treatment information to insurance companies or other funding sources.

✓ Never bill for missed sessions without being clear that no service was provided.

✓ When providing services to couples, families, or groups, ensure that the service billed accurately reflects the nature of the service provided.

✓ Never bill for psychotherapy when in fact psychological testing was provided.

✓ Never misrepresent the diagnosis or severity of any diagnosed condition.

✓ Psychologists may only bill an insurance company for a full fee and then reduce or waive the client's co-payment when allowed or authorized in the contract with the insurer.

✓ To the extent possible, protect confidential information and avoid unnecessary intrusions on privacy when reporting the nature of one's services.

✓ Remember that inaccuracy in reports to payors or funding sources harms the public perception of psychology and places you at significant risk ethically and legally.

6.07 Referrals and Fees

When psychologists pay, receive payment from, or divide fees with another professional, other than in an employer–employee relationship, the payment to each

is based on the services provided (clinical, consultative, administrative, or other) and is not based on the referral itself. (See also Standard 3.09, Cooperation With Other Professionals.)

Essential Elements

Psychologists engage clients in fiduciary relationships which imply that psychologists must act with clients' best interests at heart. When psychologists make and accept referrals or in any way share fees with others, it is imperative that clients' best interests are served. Under no circumstances is it appropriate to pay for or accept payment based on a referral itself. Such kickback arrangements may undermine a psychologist's objectivity with respect to making and accepting referrals that are clearly in the best interests of clients. The Ethics Code allows payments for referral services as long as such remuneration is based on actual services rendered.

Common Dilemmas and Conflicts

- Engaging in kickback arrangements can be tempting for psychologists in difficult financial circumstances or for psychologists who have substantial waiting lists and routinely make referrals.
- It can seem trivial or irrelevant to inform clients about any fee sharing arrangements but this should always be part of informed consent.
- Although psychologists may try to convince themselves otherwise, kickback arrangements are not in a client's best interest and are likely to have an adverse impact on the psychologist's ability to act with the client's best interests in mind.

Prevention and Positive Practice

✓ Do not pay for, or accept payment for, client referrals.
✓ If you split fees received with employees or other professionals, ensure that compensation is only for services rendered.
✓ Make any fees paid to others transparent in your informed consent process.

Standard 7. Education and Training

7.01 Design of Education and Training Programs

Psychologists responsible for education and training programs take reasonable steps to ensure that the programs are designed to provide the appropriate knowledge and proper experiences, and to meet the requirements for licensure, certification, or other goals for which claims are made by the program. (See also Standard 5.03, Descriptions of Workshops and Non-Degree-Granting Educational Programs.)

Essential Elements

When psychologists hold responsibility for designing, administering, or managing education and training programs, they have several obligations under this standard. First, psychologists ensure that academic or clinical training programs are created and implemented to deliver the knowledge, skills, and experiences required for graduates to be eligible for licensure, certification, or other goals described by the program. Second, this standard also implies that psychologists design and administer programs that are likely to contribute to competence—perhaps even excellence—among those enrolled. Finally, psychologists responsible for education and training programs are careful to ensure that their programs deliver on any explicit or implied outcomes claimed in the program's materials.

Common Dilemmas and Conflicts

- At times, institutions or organizations may exert implicit or explicit pressure on psychologists to cut corners and sacrifice quality in the design of training programs.
- It may be tempting to make students responsible for ensuring that they accumulate the experiences required for licensure or certification.
- Psychologists may feel "stuck" between leaders or administrators who limit resources while promoting questionable claims about program outcomes.

Prevention and Positive Practice

✓ When designing or administering education or training programs in psychology, be sure that the courses and experiences included meet or exceed requirements for certification, licensure, or any other outcome promised or implied.

✓ Ensure that training resources, faculty, and program components are adequate to produce competent graduates.

✓ If institutional pressure threatens the program's capacity to deliver on advertised outcomes, make your ethical obligations under this standard clear (see also Standard 1.03), and take steps to improve the program or inform those enrolled of the change.

7.02 Descriptions of Education and Training Programs

Psychologists responsible for education and training programs take reasonable steps to ensure that there is a current and accurate description of the program content (including participation in required course- or program-related counseling, psychotherapy, experiential groups, consulting projects, or community service), training goals and objectives, stipends and benefits, and requirements that must be met for satisfactory completion of the program. This information must be made readily available to all interested parties.

Essential Elements

Psychologists who have responsibility for the design or administration of education or training programs must work to ensure that any description or advertisement about the program is clear and accurate. This means that salient details regarding the program are made transparent and accessible to prospective consumers, current students, accrediting bodies, and anyone else interested in the program. Key information for inclusion in program descriptions includes training goals and objectives, graduation requirements, academic and experiential content, any stipends or benefits, costs and expenses, and the identity and credentials of faculty, supervisors, and staff. When psychologists responsible for education and training programs become aware that program descriptions are either inaccurate or inadequate, they take steps to correct the problem and inform students immediately of any change.

Common Dilemmas and Conflicts

- Because psychologists are busy and education and training programs are complicated, it may be easy to overlook inaccuracies or omissions in program descriptions.
- It is easy to downplay or disregard the fact that program descriptions constitute a form of professional advertisement (Standard 5) and an implied contract with those enrolled.
- When modifications to program requirements occur, psychologists may fail to either inform students of the change or ensure that the changes do not adversely impact students already enrolled.

Prevention and Positive Practice

- ✓ When creating, modifying, or reviewing program descriptions, describe all components and requirements clearly and accurately.
- ✓ Avoid grandiose or unfounded claims about a program's content, outcomes, or affiliated faculty.
- ✓ Treat program descriptions as an implied contract; work to fulfill the contract with those enrolled in the program.
- ✓ Demonstrate a reasonable effort to ensure that program courses and experiences actually conform to program descriptions.
- ✓ When a program description is modified, work to ensure that any discrepancies between descriptions are resolved with students' best interests at the fore.

7.03 Accuracy in Teaching

(a) Psychologists take reasonable steps to ensure that course syllabi are accurate regarding the subject matter to be covered, bases for evaluating progress, and the nature of course experiences. This standard does not preclude an instructor from modifying course content or requirements when the instructor considers it pedagogically necessary or desirable, so long as students are made aware of these modifications in a manner that enables them to fulfill course requirements. (See also Standard 5.01, Avoidance of False or Deceptive Statements.)

(b) When engaged in teaching or training, psychologists present psychological information accurately. (See also Standard 2.03, Maintaining Competence.)

Essential Elements

When teaching, psychologists prepare accurate and current course descriptions and syllabi. Syllabi should articulate key elements of the course including content to be covered, all assignments and requirements with applicable due dates, salient course experiences, criteria for evaluation and grading, and other faculty expectations. Because a syllabus constitutes a contract with students and is the basis on which students may decide to take the course, a syllabus and course should be modified only when necessary or clearly in the best interests of students. No modification should disadvantage students. Finally, psychologists have an obligation to be accurate and up-to-date with both the content covered and techniques employed in the classroom or in supervision.

Common Dilemmas and Conflicts

- The longer a psychologist teaches a course, the greater the risk that course material or descriptions may become outdated.
- When a psychologist lacks requisite experience or training, he or she may be incompetent to teach or supervise in that area (see Standard 2).
- When a psychologist fails to elaborate course content, expectations, and requirements, or when a psychologist

changes a syllabus without due regard to students' best interests, the probability of conflict with students increases.

Prevention and Positive Practice

✓ Construct both course descriptions and syllabi with attention to detail and clarity.

✓ Ask a seasoned colleague to review syllabi for omissions or inaccuracies.

✓ Maintain competence in those areas in which you teach or supervise (see Standard 2) through continuing education, reading, professional training, and scholarship.

✓ When circumstances or novel ideas precipitate a modification to the syllabus of a current course, be sure that the change does not increase the difficulty of course requirements or present added obstacles to course completion.

7.04 Student Disclosure of Personal Information

Psychologists do not require students or supervisees to disclose personal information in course- or program-related activities, either orally or in writing, regarding sexual history, history of abuse and neglect, psychological treatment, and relationships with parents, peers, and spouses or significant others except if (1) the program or training facility has clearly identified this requirement in its admissions and program materials or (2) the information is necessary to evaluate or obtain assistance for students whose personal problems could reasonably be judged to be preventing them from performing their training- or professionally related activities in a competent manner or posing a threat to the students or others.

Essential Elements

This standard and Standard 7.05 provide important safeguards for students. Although training programs have an obligation to serve as gatekeepers and ensure that students who have personal problems receive the help needed to function effectively, faculty do not have the right to require disclosures of personal information, either as a course requirement or as a result of mere curiosity. Requiring student disclosures of private information is only appropriate if the requirement is listed in the admissions and program materials or when it is apparent to the faculty member that a student may be in need of professional assistance. Faculty members must balance the obligation to address concerns with students and obtain information required to ensure remediation or treatment with the equally important obligation to respect and protect students' right to privacy.

Common Dilemmas and Conflicts

- In getting to know students, faculty may have a genuine interest in them and seek to learn more about them. However, to require disclosures of personal information solely for these reasons would be inappropriate.
- Training programs may use experiential training exercises in which students share personal information in the context of growth experiences, and yet such experiences may not be entirely transparent in admissions materials.
- Psychologists may feel ongoing tension between their evaluative and screening functions and their investment in protecting student privacy and confidentiality.

Prevention and Positive Practice

- ✓ Clearly describe any requirements for disclosure of personal information in admissions promotions, program materials, and course syllabi.
- ✓ Before seeking personal information from students for the purpose of arranging treatment or remediation, be clear that emotional or behavioral evidence is present that may interfere with the student's effective functioning or that may pose a risk to self or others.
- ✓ When possible, provide students with an alternative to experiential lab experiences or assignments requiring significant self-disclosure—perhaps with a psychologist unaffiliated with the program.

7.05 Mandatory Individual or Group Therapy

(a) **When individual or group therapy is a program or course requirement, psychologists responsible for that program allow students in undergraduate and graduate programs the option of selecting such ther-**

apy from practitioners unaffiliated with the program.
(See also Standard 7.02, Descriptions of Education
and Training Programs.)

(b) Faculty who are or are likely to be responsible for
evaluating students' academic performance do not
themselves provide that therapy. (See also Standard
3.05, Multiple Relationships.)

Essential Elements

Undergraduate and graduate students may participate in a range
of experiential clinical training experiences as part of their education. When individual or group psychotherapy are components
of the training program's requirements, students are afforded
the option of seeking this treatment from psychotherapists who
are not affiliated with their graduate program and who do not
have evaluative authority over the students. Even when students
participate in such psychotherapy experiences in their own program, the psychotherapists should not also be responsible for the
students' academic evaluation. This dual role would constitute a
clear conflict of interest for the faculty and place the students in
an untenable situation.

Common Dilemmas and Conflicts

- Faculty with expertise in psychotherapy may be tempted
  to provide in vivo experiences to students as a part of their
  professional training, perhaps assuming that the roles of
  psychotherapist and faculty member can be separated
  effectively.
- It is often difficult to predict how the roles of psychotherapist and faculty evaluator may become incompatible or
  conflicted.
- Psychotherapy with trainees may elicit evidence of impairment that the faculty member may feel compelled to
  address administratively, thus creating a harmful multiple
  relationship for the student.

Prevention and Positive Practice

✓ Remember that your evaluative and gatekeeper roles prevent you from serving effectively in the role of psychotherapist to students.

✓ Afford students the option to receive psychotherapy experiences from clinicians not affiliated with the training program.

✓ When students elect to meet psychotherapy or experiential requirements outside the program, it is appropriate to seek verification that the requirement was met.

7.06 Assessing Student and Supervisee Performance

(a) In academic and supervisory relationships, psychologists establish a timely and specific process for providing feedback to students and supervisees. Information regarding the process is provided to the student at the beginning of supervision.

(b) Psychologists evaluate students and supervisees on the basis of their actual performance on relevant and established program requirements.

Essential Elements

Psychologists serving in faculty and supervisor roles must provide timely, relevant, and helpful evaluation and feedback to students and supervisees. Specific information regarding how evaluation will be conducted is shared in the course syllabus and in the informed consent to supervision process. Students and supervisees must be evaluated on criteria of direct relevance to the material and skills they are learning. Supervisors must provide supervisees with timely feedback that allows them to take needed steps to correct deficiencies. Evaluation and feedback are best provided in writing and discussed with supervisees periodically throughout the training experience in addition to informal feedback that should be provided on an ongoing basis.

Common Dilemmas and Conflicts

- Supervisors may feel that informal feedback is sufficient because clinical supervision is different from teaching in the classroom.
- It may be tempting to allow personal reactions to students and supervisees or personal biases to impact the evaluative statements psychologists make.

- It is easy to assume that students and supervisees implicitly understand evaluation criteria, making it unnecessary to discuss them at the beginning of the professional relationship.

Prevention and Positive Practice

✓ Share and discuss clear standards for evaluation—including objective criteria—at the outset of every teaching and supervision relationship.

✓ Make evaluation criteria relevant to the goals of the education or training experience.

✓ Establish a clear schedule for formal written evaluation and feedback at the outset of the professional relationship. Provide feedback throughout the training experience.

✓ Make feedback helpful to the trainee; include suggestions for corrective actions needed to remediate any deficiencies.

7.07 Sexual Relationships With Students and Supervisees

Psychologists do not engage in sexual relationships with students or supervisees who are in their department, agency, or training center or over whom psychologists have or are likely to have evaluative authority. (See also Standard 3.05, Multiple Relationships.)

Essential Elements

Similar to the admonition against intimate relationships with current clients and patients, psychologists never engage in sexual relationships with their students and supervisees. There are several reasons why sexual relationships with students and supervisees are never appropriate: (a) the inherent imbalance of power in the relationship, (b) its evaluative nature, (c) the need for objectivity in evaluating trainees, (d) students' and supervisees' dependence on teachers and trust that they will only act with students' best interests in mind, and (e) the real potential for exploitation and harm resulting from sexual involvement. Additionally, sexual liaisons between psychologists and trainees contaminate the academic environment, adversely impact the image of the profession with the public, and provide poor role modeling to students and supervisees.

Common Dilemmas and Conflicts

- Faculty and supervisors may work closely with students and supervisees for long hours. It may be tempting to allow the relationship to take on a romantic flavor.
- Mentoring may be an aspect of these relationships, and the intimate and close personal contact present may make it easy to cross over into inappropriate roles.
- The self-disclosure and mutual attraction common to many good advising, mentoring, and supervision relationships may place both parties at risk for the development of a more intimate relationship.
- It may be easy to interpret such a relationship as special and to act on this inappropriately.

Prevention and Positive Practice

- ✓ Establish clear and consistent boundaries, remain cognizant of the trust placed in you by the profession and by subordinates, and always keep students' and supervisees' best interests in mind.
- ✓ Carefully monitor your attitudes, thoughts, and feelings about trainees. If you begin seeing a particular student or supervisee as special and begin considering a romantic or sexual relationship, immediately seek consultation and supervision.
- ✓ Remember your obligations as a role model for those you supervise and train.
- ✓ Never take actions that are likely to impair your objectivity and judgment.

Standard 8. Research and Publication

8.01 Institutional Approval

When institutional approval is required, psychologists provide accurate information about their research proposals and obtain approval prior to conducting the research. They conduct the research in accordance with the approved research protocol.

Essential Elements

As researchers, psychologists always obtain necessary institutional approval before initiating any study. In their applications to institutional review boards and other entities psychologists are fully truthful in all information provided about the design and procedures of their study. When approval is granted, psychologists carefully ensure that the study is carried out in full compliance with the approved protocol.

Common Dilemmas and Conflicts

- Psychologists under pressure to achieve promotion or secure grant funding may be at risk of cutting corners in this area.
- Pressures to carry out research in a timely manner may push psychologists to begin research projects prior to institutional approval being granted.

- A desire to have one's research proposal approved may result in withholding or fabricating crucial information in application materials.
- Various pressures may result in a failure to comply with the approved research protocol.

Prevention and Positive Practice

✓ Never conduct research without first obtaining all needed institutional approvals.

✓ Openly and fully disclose all relevant information in applications for approval, and assiduously follow all requirements set in the approval.

✓ Acknowledge the institutional approval process as an important safeguard ensuring ethical and effective research, not as a burden or obstacle to be resisted.

8.02 Informed Consent to Research

(a) When obtaining informed consent as required in Standard 3.10, Informed Consent, psychologists inform participants about (1) the purpose of the research, expected duration, and procedures; (2) their right to decline to participate and to withdraw from the research once participation has begun; (3) the foreseeable consequences of declining or withdrawing; (4) reasonably foreseeable factors that may be expected to influence their willingness to participate such as potential risks, discomfort, or adverse effects; (5) any prospective research benefits; (6) limits of confidentiality; (7) incentives for participation; and (8) whom to contact for questions about the research and research participants' rights. They provide opportunity for the prospective participants to ask questions and receive answers. (See also Standards 8.03, Informed Consent for Recording Voices and Images in Research; 8.05, Dispensing With Informed Consent for Research; and 8.07, Deception in Research.)

(b) Psychologists conducting intervention research involving the use of experimental treatments clarify to participants at the outset of the research (1) the experimental nature of the treatment; (2) the services that will or will not be available to the control group(s) if appropriate; (3) the means by which assignment to treatment and control groups will be made; (4) available treatment alternatives if an individual does not wish to participate in the research or wishes to withdraw once a study has begun; and (5) compensation for or monetary costs of participating including, if appropriate, whether reimbursement from the participant or a third-party payor will be sought. (See also Standard 8.02a, Informed Consent to Research.)

Essential Elements

This standard specifies the information that must be shared and issues to be addressed in every informed consent agreement for research participation. This information is shared with prospective research participants to ensure that each participant's rights are respected and to ensure that he or she has adequate information to make an informed decision about participation. In addition to providing each of the key components of informed consent to research, participants must be given the opportunity to ask questions, and researchers must provide complete and honest answers. Concern for the protection of each research participant's rights should guide this process. When conducting intervention research that involves the use of experimental treatments, psychologists must provide additional information about the nature of these treatments as detailed in this standard. Additional issues addressed include the experimental nature of the treatment, services available or not available to those in control groups, how treatment condition assignments are made, treatment alternatives for those who decline participation in the study or who withdraw from it, compensation or costs for participation, and who is responsible for any fees charged.

Common Dilemmas and Conflicts

- Researchers under pressure to ensure adequate participation in their study may be tempted to dispense with informed consent or to share insufficient information to potential participants.

- Those providing experimental treatments may assume that all potential participants understand the relative risks and benefits involved and do not need careful explanations of all the issues that might impact a decision to participate.

Prevention and Positive Practice

✓ Always engage in a comprehensive informed consent agreement with all prospective research participants and ensure their understanding before including them in the study.

✓ Only conduct studies involving experimental treatments after careful review of factors that might impact an individual's decision to participate.

✓ Never assume that prospective participants understand informed consent; always ensure full informed consent prior to participation.

8.03 Informed Consent for Recording Voices and Images in Research

Psychologists obtain informed consent from research participants prior to recording their voices or images for data collection unless (1) the research consists solely of naturalistic observations in public places, and it is not anticipated that the recording will be used in a manner that could cause personal identification or harm, or (2) the research design includes deception, and consent for the use of the recording is obtained during debriefing. (See also Standard 8.07, Deception in Research.)

Essential Elements

When using audio and video recording as part of a research study, psychologists must protect each participant's privacy rights. Except for the two situations to be described, psychologists first obtain research subjects' permission as part of the informed consent process. This informed consent would include both the nature and use of the recorded information. This requirement may be waived in the case of naturalistic observation in public places as long as the recordings will not be used in a manner that could cause personal identification or harm. Further, if the use of recording is part of the deception used in research, each participant's informed consent to use the recordings must be obtained during the debriefing at the conclusion of the study.

Common Dilemmas and Conflicts

- Using audio and video recordings in research may seem like excellent ways to collect data for later analysis and review. However, to violate participants' privacy rights and to assume their willingness to be recorded would be inappropriate.
- Simply because a study involves naturalistic observation versus manipulation of variables is insufficient reason to dispense with informed consent if there is any chance a participant could be identified or harmed as a result of audio or video recording.
- Those using deception in research may erroneously assume that deception eliminates the requirement for informed consent prior to using the recordings as part of a study.

Prevention and Positive Practice

- ✓ Always ensure that research participants' rights are respected; obtain consent to record research participants whenever necessary.
- ✓ Even with naturalistic observation in public places, be sure that privacy rights are not violated and that harm to participants does not occur.
- ✓ When deception is used in a study, be sure that the use of recordings is addressed fully in the debriefing process and that participants understand their right to refuse to have the recordings used in the study.

8.04 Client/Patient, Student, and Subordinate Research Participants

(a) When psychologists conduct research with clients/ patients, students, or subordinates as participants, psychologists take steps to protect the prospective participants from adverse consequences of declining or withdrawing from participation.

(b) When research participation is a course requirement or an opportunity for extra credit, the prospective participant is given the choice of equitable alternative activities.

Essential Elements

Psychologist researchers bear a great responsibility to protect the best interests of those they study and take care not to exploit them in any way. When clients or patients, students, or subordinates participate in research, psychologists take special precautions to ensure that no coercion occurs and that anyone may decline participation in research without any untoward consequences. Psychologists must appreciate any imbalance of power and be sure they do not take advantage of it. When participation in research is a course requirement, students must be offered alternatives that are similar in their time commitment and other demands. Students should never be forced to participate in a research study, and the faculty member's power over the student should not be misused.

Common Dilemmas and Conflicts

- Pressures to obtain a suitable sample size in a research project may result in exerting pressure on individuals who trust psychologists not to take advantage of their relative power.
- It is easy to forget that clients or patients, students, and subordinates may not feel comfortable declining a request to participate in research because of fear of adverse consequences if they do.
- Although faculty may believe that participation in a study will be an excellent training experience for students, requiring this would possibly exploit students and violate their rights.

Prevention and Positive Practice

✓ Always ensure that all potential research subjects understand that their participation is voluntary and ensure their right to refuse participation without penalty.

✓ Be aware of the imbalance of power present in professional relationships and the trust that patients or clients, students, and subordinates have in psychologists not to take advantage of it.

✓ Always offer students reasonable options and alternatives to participation in research studies when this is a course requirement.

8.05 Dispensing With Informed Consent for Research

Psychologists may dispense with informed consent only (1) where research would not reasonably be assumed to create distress or harm and involves (a) the study of normal educational practices, curricula, or classroom management methods conducted in educational settings; (b) only anonymous questionnaires, naturalistic observations, or archival research for which disclosure of responses would not place participants at risk of criminal or civil liability or damage their financial standing, employability, or reputation, and confidentiality is protected; or (c) the study of factors related to job or organization effectiveness conducted in organizational settings for which there is no risk to participants' employability, and confidentiality is protected or (2) where otherwise permitted by law or federal or institutional regulations.

Essential Elements

Despite the great importance of informed consent, there are times when it is appropriate not to engage in an informed consent process when conducting research. Specific situations that do not require consent include (a) studies of classroom management methods and normal educational practices in which no reasonable assumption of harm exists and (b) studies using questionnaires, naturalistic observation, or archival research methods in which rights of anonymity are protected and risks of harm are minimal. Additionally, consent is not needed when studying job or organizational effectiveness in organizational settings and when there is no risk to participants and their confidentiality is protected. Finally, psychologists may dispense with informed consent when permitted by law or regulation.

Common Dilemmas and Conflicts

- It is easy to underestimate the actual risks to research participants and not take adequate precautions to protect their rights.
- Assuming that informed consent is not needed without considering the factors detailed in the previous section may place participants at risk.
- Those unfamiliar with the specifics of law and federal and institutional regulations may be at risk of dispensing with informed consent inappropriately.

Prevention and Positive Practice

- ✓ Only dispense with informed consent after thoughtful consideration of each of the factors in this standard.
- ✓ Take special care to ensure that each research participant's rights are respected and upheld.
- ✓ Know the laws and applicable regulations when making decisions about using or dispensing with informed consent in research.

8.06 Offering Inducements for Research Participation

(a) **Psychologists make reasonable efforts to avoid offering excessive or inappropriate financial or other inducements for research participation when such inducements are likely to coerce participation.**

(b) **When offering professional services as an inducement for research participation, psychologists clarify the nature of the services, as well as the risks, obligations, and limitations. (See also Standard 6.05, Barter With Clients/Patients.)**

Essential Elements

Psychologists frequently offer inducements to potential research subjects to encourage their participation in a study. Examples include entering participants in a raffle, paying them an agreed-on fee, or providing them with certain health and mental health services. Psychologist researchers must ensure that potential research participants are not exploited and that inducements do not take advantage of their vulnerabilities. Any coercion to participate in research with offers "too good to refuse" are considered inappropriate. When services are offered to compensate for participation in a study, psychologists provide informed consent and carefully address the nature of the services to be provided and all risks, obligations, and limitations so that participants have realistic expectations about the proposed services and their likely outcomes.

Common Dilemmas and Conflicts

- In an effort to procure an adequate sample size it may be tempting to offer inducements for participation that are excessive, exploitative, or coercive in nature.
- Psychologists who work with vulnerable populations such as inpatients, prisoners, children, and the impoverished may overlook vulnerabilities to coercive influence in those they serve.

Prevention and Positive Practice

✓ Always take precautions to ensure that vulnerable individuals are not coerced or exploited. When unsure, consult with a colleague not affiliated with your study.
✓ Inducements to participate in research should be comparable in value to the time and commitment required for participating in the study.
✓ When services are provided be sure that fully informed consent is provided first so that realistic expectations are held by all involved.

8.07 Deception in Research

   (a) Psychologists do not conduct a study involving deception unless they have determined that the use of deceptive techniques is justified by the study's significant prospective scientific, educational, or applied value and that effective nondeceptive alternative procedures are not feasible.

   (b) Psychologists do not deceive prospective participants about research that is reasonably expected to cause physical pain or severe emotional distress.

   (c) **Psychologists explain any deception that is an integral feature of the design and conduct of an experiment to participants as early as is feasible, preferably at the conclusion of their participation, but no later than at the conclusion of the data collection, and permit participants to withdraw their data. (See also Standard 8.08, Debriefing.)**

Essential Elements

At times the use of deception is the only way to conduct an important study, and without the use of deception there would be no way to advance knowledge and understanding in a particular area. But, when using deception great care must be taken. It is essential that deception only be used when no reasonable alternative exists and the potential benefits of the research are sufficient to warrant using deception. Deception is never to be used when there is a risk of physical pain or severe emotional distress occurring as a result of participation in the study. When deception is used it must be explained to participants at the earliest possible time, but no later than at the conclusion of data collection. When this debriefing occurs psychologists must allow participants the option of withdrawing their data from the study should they so choose.

Common Dilemmas and Conflicts

- Because of the perceived value of studies involving deception, researchers may overlook other options and risk unnecessary harm to participants.
- Excitement about the potential for advancement of knowledge and understanding of important phenomena may result in researchers placing participants at risk for physical harm or emotional suffering without adequate justification.
- A fear of participants withdrawing their data in response to learning they were deceived may place researchers at risk of minimizing or avoiding the debriefing process.

Prevention and Positive Practice

✓ Only use deception in research when no other reasonable alternative exists and when the potential value of the research findings is significant.

✓ Actively seek creative alternatives to the use of deception.

✓ Thoroughly consider the risks of harm and suffering to participants; avoid deception if significant risks exist.

✓ Thoughtfully and openly debrief participants who have been deceived in a research study, and offer participants the option of withdrawing their data.

✓ Be certain that an appropriate institutional review board approves the use of deception before collecting any data in this way.

8.08 Debriefing

(a) Psychologists provide a prompt opportunity for participants to obtain appropriate information about the nature, results, and conclusions of the research, and they take reasonable steps to correct any misconceptions that participants may have of which the psychologists are aware.

(b) If scientific or humane values justify delaying or withholding this information, psychologists take reasonable measures to reduce the risk of harm.

(c) When psychologists become aware that research procedures have harmed a participant, they take reasonable steps to minimize the harm.

Essential Elements

Whenever possible, research participants should be fully informed about the nature and purpose of the study. In most cases, thorough debriefing will include the real purpose of the research, the nature of any deception, the potential effects—if any—of the deception, and the results and conclusions of the study as soon as these are available. At times an institutional review board may approve a protocol that includes deception or other manipulation of participants' perceptions of a study for some valid scientific purpose. When this occurs, psychologists make great effort to debrief participants immediately following data collection. Unless debriefing would be inappropriate for some reason (e.g., prone to cause greater harm to the participant), it should occur anytime participants do not have complete information about the nature or purpose of the research in advance. Finally, psychologists must be vigilant for any evidence that a research participant was harmed in any way by the study and take whatever steps are needed to ameliorate the negative effects and reduce the risk of additional harm.

Common Dilemmas and Conflicts

- Psychologists who are busy and pressed by research deadlines may be tempted to ignore evidence of distress in participants or to bypass the time-consuming process of debriefing.
- Unless the entire informed consent process has been waived, there is rarely appropriate justification for failing to debrief participants who have been deceived in some way.
- It is easy to promise participants a summary of the results and harder to follow through with this.

Prevention and Positive Practice

- ✓ Always debrief research participants regarding the nature and results of any study you conduct; this is essential when deception has been employed.
- ✓ Be sure to explain the rationale for any deception after data collection is complete, and remain sensitive to any distress or harm this might cause the participant.
- ✓ Make debriefing an ongoing process; allow participants to contact you regarding any concern even after the study is complete.
- ✓ Intervene actively if a participant shows signs of distress or reports harm arising from a research study, and make thorough efforts to reduce distress and prevent further harm.

8.09 Humane Care and Use of Animals in Research

(a) Psychologists acquire, care for, use, and dispose of animals in compliance with current federal, state, and local laws and regulations, and with professional standards.

(b) Psychologists trained in research methods and experienced in the care of laboratory animals supervise all procedures involving animals and are responsible for ensuring appropriate consideration of their comfort, health, and humane treatment.

(c) Psychologists ensure that all individuals under their supervision who are using animals have received instruction in research methods and in the care, maintenance, and handling of the species being used, to the extent appropriate to their role. (See also Standard 2.05, Delegation of Work to Others.)

(d) Psychologists make reasonable efforts to minimize the discomfort, infection, illness, and pain of animal subjects.

(e) Psychologists use a procedure subjecting animals to pain, stress, or privation only when an alternative procedure is unavailable and the goal is justified by its prospective scientific, educational, or applied value.

(f) Psychologists perform surgical procedures under appropriate anesthesia and follow techniques to avoid infection and minimize pain during and after surgery.

(g) When it is appropriate that an animal's life be terminated, psychologists proceed rapidly, with an effort to minimize pain and in accordance with accepted procedures.

Essential Elements

Psychologists involved in the acquisition, care, use of, and disposal of animals in research or educational contexts ensure they are competent in the appropriate and humane care and use of animals for these purposes, and they also comply with all relevant laws and regulations bearing on the care and treatment of animals. When using animals for any purpose, psychologists attempt to minimize distress and harm, use the least invasive experimental techniques possible, and use appropriate anesthesia practices when surgery is required. Psychologists are attentive to both legal requirements and professional standards bearing on the use of animals, and they work to ensure that all colleagues, employees, supervisees, and students also abide by these standards. When a research animal's life must be terminated, psychologists must carefully adhere to accepted procedures and make every effort to minimize pain or distress for the animal. Finally, all subordinates who have such duties delegated to them must first be appropriately trained and then must be sufficiently supervised to ensure that the specifics of this standard are always followed.

Common Dilemmas and Conflicts

- Psychologists who are not appropriately trained or supervised in the appropriate care of research animals may be at risk of incompetent and unethical behavior in this area.
- Psychologists unfamiliar with current standards for the acquisition, care, use, and disposal of animals may be at risk in this area.
- Psychologists who inappropriately delegate animal care to persons without careful training and supervision may be at risk in this area.

Prevention and Positive Practice

- ✓ Ensure your competence to work with research animals by securing appropriate education, training, and supervision in this area.
- ✓ Be thoroughly familiar with the latest version of the American Psychological Association's (APA's) Guidelines for Ethical Conduct in the Care and Use of Animals (http://www.apa.org/science/anguide.html).
- ✓ Become familiar with local, state, and federal laws bearing on the acquisition, care, use of, and disposal of animals and ensure your own and your subordinates' adherence to these laws.
- ✓ Consult the U.S. Department of Agriculture's Animal Welfare Guidelines (http://www.aphis.usda.gov/animal_welfare/index.shtml).
- ✓ Carefully train and supervise any employee or student who will work with research animals on your behalf.
- ✓ Always seek to minimize distress, pain, and needless suffering in any animal under your care.

8.10 Reporting Research Results

(a) **Psychologists do not fabricate data. (See also Standard 5.01a, Avoidance of False or Deceptive Statements.)**

(b) If psychologists discover significant errors in their published data, they take reasonable steps to correct such errors in a correction, retraction, erratum, or other appropriate publication means.

Essential Elements

Although psychologists may occasionally face pressure to modify or even falsify data to achieve a specific result, this constitutes scientific misconduct and is never acceptable. Psychologists must assiduously avoid any inaccuracy in the data they collect and findings they report. Faking or otherwise presenting data inaccurately may directly or indirectly harm the public by erroneously influencing public behavior, available treatments, future research, or public policy. When a psychologist becomes aware of an error in something he or she has published, the psychologist takes reasonable steps to make sure the public is informed of this error. This typically involves requesting that the publication outlet publish a brief correction.

Common Dilemmas and Conflicts

- Psychologists or graduate students feeling significant pressure to secure grant funding, achieve promotion and tenure, or complete degree requirements may find data fraud more tempting.
- Psychologists who are extremely ambitious and competitive may be at greater risk in this area.
- When significant results are required for publication, the temptation to fake, tamper with, or selectively include data increases.
- Psychologists may minimize the significance of errors in their published work in articles or media coverage, thereby failing to take appropriate corrective measures.

Prevention and Positive Practice

✓ Refuse to falsify data or present data in such a way as to mislead.
✓ Remind yourself that it would be better to fail to achieve funding, promotion, tenure, or graduation than to be charged with scientific misconduct.

✓ Immediately notify a publisher when you become aware that a significant error in your data has been published, and clearly request a correction, retraction, erratum, or other appropriate fix.

8.11 Plagiarism

Psychologists do not present portions of another's work or data as their own, even if the other work or data source is cited occasionally.

Essential Elements

It is never acceptable for a psychologist to present someone else's work as his or her own either explicitly or by implication. The ideas of others must be credited, and direct quotations from other authors must be carefully cited. The prohibition against plagiarism covers presenting others' work in any medium, and the motivation for plagiarism is irrelevant. Plagiarism violates Principle C: Integrity and often causes harm to persons whose work is taken without due credit.

Common Dilemmas and Conflicts

- Graduate students and inexperienced psychologists may be most likely to inaccurately or inadequately cite the work of others.
- Students and psychologists feeling significant pressure to complete degree requirements or achieve promotion may be most tempted to plagiarize.
- Authors working under pressure to meet deadlines and who are not organized may inadvertently use others' ideas and work without proper attribution.

Prevention and Positive Practice

✓ Be familiar with the section of the APA *Publication Manual*[1] bearing on the citation of others' work.

---

[1]American Psychological Association. (2001). *Publication manual of the American Psychological Association* (5th ed.). Washington, DC: Author.

✓ Always credit previous ideas or findings to the original authors; give credit by citing the author when you paraphrase others' work; and cite specific page numbers when you directly quote others' work.

✓ Carefully organize materials before starting to write so that the work of other authors can be correctly attributed.

✓ Be alert to the possibility of unintentional plagiarism.

8.12 Publication Credit

(a) Psychologists take responsibility and credit, including authorship credit, only for work they have actually performed or to which they have substantially contributed. (See also Standard 8.12b, Publication Credit.)

(b) Principal authorship and other publication credits accurately reflect the relative scientific or professional contributions of the individuals involved, regardless of their relative status. Mere possession of an institutional position, such as department chair, does not justify authorship credit. Minor contributions to the research or to the writing for publications are acknowledged appropriately, such as in footnotes or in an introductory statement.

(c) Except under exceptional circumstances, a student is listed as principal author on any multiple-authored article that is substantially based on the student's doctoral dissertation. Faculty advisors discuss publication credit with students as early as feasible and throughout the research and publication process as appropriate. (See also Standard 8.12b, Publication Credit.)

Essential Elements

Few issues create more tension or more frequent ethical complaints in academic settings than disputes over authorship and publication credit. Integrity (Principle C) requires that psychologists accurately portray their own contributions and those of others in any project in which they are involved. It is never appropriate to accept responsibility or credit for work to which one has not significantly contributed. Further, order of authorship on any multiauthored work should accurately reflect the work completed by each member of the writing or research team. A psychologist's status and position should not impact decisions about authorship. Presentations and publications based primarily on a student's dissertation should list the student as first author unless there is some extraordinary circumstance. Because issues of authorship and publication credit have the potential to create so much acrimony, it is incumbent on psychologists working with writing or research teams or with students to make authorship and publication credit part of an ongoing informed consent process.

Common Dilemmas and Conflicts

- Psychologists who are particularly ambitious, entitled, or prone to overestimate their contributions may stumble in this area.
- New psychologists struggling to achieve tenure and promotion may be more inclined to take credit for work they have not performed.
- Senior psychologists may be tempted to demand authorship on student projects when authorship has not been earned.
- In an effort to assist a colleague or student, a psychologist may inappropriately offer publication credit without the requisite contribution.

Prevention and Positive Practice

- ✓ Make publication credit and authorship decisions part of an ongoing informed consent process (see Standard 3.10) when engaging in research and scholarship.
- ✓ Come to terms with coauthors—including students—regarding publication credit and order of authorship before commencing any scholarly project. Recognize minor contributions with footnotes or introductory acknowledgments.
- ✓ Remain flexible regarding authorship and publication credit; as circumstances and workloads shift, revisit these issues so that each contributor's work is appropriately credited.
- ✓ Remember that graduate students should always be first author on products based on their dissertation (unless very atypical circumstances warrant a different arrangement);

faculty must be cautious to avoid any coercion or exploitation (see Standard 3.08) of students' work.

✓ If a disagreement regarding authorship credit arises, consider asking a neutral colleague to arbitrate and objectively weigh each person's relative contributions.

8.13 Duplicate Publication of Data

Psychologists do not publish, as original data, data that have been previously published. This does not preclude republishing data when they are accompanied by proper acknowledgment.

Essential Elements

It is not ethical to publish data more than once unless the editor or publisher is clearly informed at the outset and the previous publication is clearly acknowledged in the second publication. Editors, publishers, the broader scientific community, and the public share an expectation that all published work is original unless otherwise indicated.

Common Dilemmas and Conflicts

- Psychologists feeling pressure to publish or perish in academe may be tempted to engage in duplicate or fragmented publication of their work.
- It is tempting to inflate one's list of publications by publishing multiple works based on a single study.

Prevention and Positive Practice

✓ Never submit the same work for publication in more than one outlet at a time, and never submit previously published work as though it were original.

✓ Clearly inform the editor or publisher at the outset if you plan to submit more than one manuscript based on a single study.

8.14 Sharing Research Data for Verification

(a) After research results are published, psychologists do not withhold the data on which their conclusions

are based from other competent professionals who seek to verify the substantive claims through re-analysis and who intend to use such data only for that purpose, provided that the confidentiality of the participants can be protected and unless legal rights concerning proprietary data preclude their release. This does not preclude psychologists from requiring that such individuals or groups be responsible for costs associated with the provision of such information.

(b) Psychologists who request data from other psychologists to verify the substantive claims through reanalysis may use shared data only for the declared purpose. Requesting psychologists obtain prior written agreement for all other uses of the data.

Essential Elements

Psychologists who engage in research and publication of research results hold an obligation to make their data available to others for the purpose of scrutiny and verification. When another professional requests data from published results, psychologists are required by this standard to release the data provided that (a) the person requesting the data has reasonable competence in the field, (b) participant confidentiality can be protected, (c) legal rights concerning the data do not prevent their release, and (d) the professional requesting the data intends to use them only for the purpose of reanalysis or verification of results. When psychologists request data from other researchers for the purpose of verification, they use the data only for this purpose and do not publish or otherwise disseminate the data without written agreement from the original researcher.

Common Dilemmas and Conflicts

- Psychologists who become defensive or distrusting when another professional requests data for verification purposes may experience difficulty complying with this standard.
- Psychologists who fail to archive data for a reasonable period of time following publication may be at risk of violating this standard.

■ Psychologists who comply with verification requests without first ensuring that participant confidentiality can be protected and that no legal constraint prevents such release may have trouble in this area.

Prevention and Positive Practice

✓ Fight the temptation to become angry or defensive when another professional requests data for verification purposes.
✓ Verify that participant confidentiality can be protected before releasing original data.
✓ If data are likely to be requested by other professionals, make this part of the informed consent process with research participants and employ coding or other strategies to protect participants' identities.

8.15 Reviewers

Psychologists who review material submitted for presentation, publication, grant, or research proposal review respect the confidentiality of and the proprietary rights in such information of those who submitted it.

Essential Elements

When psychologists have the privilege of reviewing colleagues' work on behalf of a professional journal, publisher, conference committee, or funding source, it is essential that they respect the confidentiality of the information; reviewing psychologists refrain from disseminating or using the authors' ideas or findings without appropriate consent from the authors and without accurately crediting the authors (see Standard 8.11).

Common Dilemmas and Conflicts

■ Reviewing psychologists are often active scholars themselves; it can be difficult to encounter fresh and exciting ideas in the reviewer role while simultaneously respecting confidentiality and avoiding mention of these ideas in one's own writing.
■ Careless reviewers may subtly incorporate confidential work into their own scholarship or cite confidential work without the original authors' permission.

Prevention and Positive Practice

✓ Protect the confidentiality of any manuscript, presentation proposal, or grant application with the same rigor you might protect a client's clinical record.

✓ Destroy the original manuscript or application when your review is completed.

✓ Never use or cite the original ideas or findings of an author whose work you have reviewed without first securing explicit permission from that author.

✓ Remind yourself that until a work you have reviewed has been published or otherwise introduced into the public domain, you must avoid taking any advantage of your prior knowledge of the work.

Standard 9. Assessment

9.01 Bases for Assessments

(a) Psychologists base the opinions contained in their recommendations, reports, and diagnostic or evaluative statements, including forensic testimony, on information and techniques sufficient to substantiate their findings. (See also Standard 2.04, Bases for Scientific and Professional Judgments.)

(b) Except as noted in 9.01c, psychologists provide opinions of the psychological characteristics of individuals only after they have conducted an examination of the individuals adequate to support their statements or conclusions. When, despite reasonable efforts, such an examination is not practical, psychologists document the efforts they made and the result of those efforts, clarify the probable impact of their limited information on the reliability and validity of their opinions, and appropriately limit the nature and extent of their conclusions or recommendations. (See also Standards 2.01, Boundaries of Competence, and 9.06, Interpreting Assessment Results.)

(c) When psychologists conduct a record review or provide consultation or supervision and an individual examination is not warranted or necessary for the opinion, psychologists explain this and the sources

of information on which they based their conclusions and recommendations.

Essential Elements

Psychologists recognize that assessment results often have significant consequences for those assessed. Psychologists must limit
their assessment services to those evaluation procedures, psychological tests, and areas of assessment for which they have developed competence through appropriate training, supervision, and
experience. It is imperative that psychologists who engage in
assessment have a reasonable understanding of psychometric
principles, including standardization, reliability, and validity,
especially as they apply to individual clients. Competent psychologists insist on interviewing those they assess, reviewing
previous records when available, and carefully interpreting individual test results in light of client and contextual variables.
Psychologists should always convey any concern about the reliability or validity of their assessments and err on the side of
caution in making diagnoses or recommendations based on
assessment results. When psychologists offer a record review or
consultation without conducting an in-person interview, they
clarify this omission and its implications for the validity of their
conclusions.

Common Dilemmas and Conflicts

- Psychologists who are pressed for time or concerned about
  lack of reimbursement for assessment procedures may be
  tempted to (a) skip indicated assessment procedures altogether or (b) engage in fraud by billing assessment procedures as though they were treatment (see Standard 5.01,
  Avoidance of False or Deceptive Statements).
- In an effort to expedite assessment, psychologists may dispense with personal interviews, allow clients to take testing
  materials home, or accept computer-generated interpretive
  reports without their own contextual interpretation.
- As a result of incompetence, bias, or efforts to please a
  client or third party, psychologists may be tempted to
  overstate the accuracy or predictive value of assessment
  results.

Prevention and Positive Practice

✓ Be sure to note any concerns about the reliability or validity of a client's assessment results due to client (e.g., fatigue, anxiety, language) or context (e.g., lighting, interruptions) factors.

✓ Be very familiar with the American Psychological Association's (APA's) Standards for Educational and Psychological Testing (2000; http://www.apa.org/science/standards.html).

✓ Never interpret test results for someone you have not personally interviewed without noting this.

✓ Remember to request previous assessment and treatment records before conducting an assessment, and always consider medical factors.

✓ Only use assessment instruments for those purposes for which they are valid.

✓ Recognize the limits of certainty in your conclusions and recommendations; communicate these limitations clearly.

9.02 Use of Assessments

(a) Psychologists administer, adapt, score, interpret, or use assessment techniques, interviews, tests, or instruments in a manner and for purposes that are appropriate in light of the research on or evidence of the usefulness and proper application of the techniques.

(b) Psychologists use assessment instruments whose validity and reliability have been established for use with members of the population tested. When such validity or reliability has not been established, psychologists describe the strengths and limitations of test results and interpretation.

(c) Psychologists use assessment methods that are appropriate to an individual's language preference and competence, unless the use of an alternative language is relevant to the assessment issues.

Essential Elements

Psychologists are careful to use tests and other assessment techniques in a manner and for those purposes for which they are appropriate given the publisher's standardization instructions and the empirical evidence of the technique's usefulness. Psychologists are especially thoughtful about the standardization of psychological instruments and their reliability and validity with specific groups and for specific purposes. Because misuse of assessment procedures can harm or disadvantage clients and diminish the pubic perception of psychology as a profession, psychologists are careful in the selection and interpretation of psychological tests. Finally, psychologists actively consider client culture, language, race, ethnicity, gender, age, physical disability, and other variables in determining the most valid and appropriate approach to assessment and the interpretation of assessment results.

Common Dilemmas and Conflicts

- Psychologists who fail to consider the impact of cultural variables when conducting an assessment are at risk in this area.
- Psychologists who make diagnostic conclusions or recommendations based on outdated materials, obsolete techniques, or tests with poor or unknown validity are at risk in this area.

Prevention and Positive Practice

- ✓ Ensure that you are competent to administer, score, and interpret any instrument you employ in conducting assessments.
- ✓ Do not allow employees, assistants, or supervisees to administer or score tests without appropriate training and oversight.
- ✓ Base assessments on up-to-date and valid techniques.
- ✓ When an assessment instrument is administered in a nonstandard fashion, clarify this in your report and indicate how this may impact validity or reliability.
- ✓ Always consider the implications of the APA's Guidelines for Providers of Psychological Services to Ethnic, Linguistic, and Culturally Diverse Populations (http://www.apa.org/pi/oema/guide.html).

9.03 Informed Consent in Assessments

(a) Psychologists obtain informed consent for assessments, evaluations, or diagnostic services, as described in Standard 3.10, Informed Consent, except when (1) testing is mandated by law or governmental regulations; (2) informed consent is implied because testing is conducted as a routine educational, institutional, or organizational activity (e.g., when participants voluntarily agree to assessment when applying for a job); or (3) one purpose of the testing is to evaluate decisional capacity. Informed consent includes an explanation of the nature and purpose of the assessment, fees, involvement of third parties, and limits of confidentiality and sufficient opportunity for the client/patient to ask questions and receive answers.

(b) Psychologists inform persons with questionable capacity to consent or for whom testing is mandated by law or governmental regulations about the nature and purpose of the proposed assessment services, using language that is reasonably understandable to the person being assessed.

(c) Psychologists using the services of an interpreter obtain informed consent from the client/patient to use that interpreter, ensure that confidentiality of test results and test security are maintained, and include in their recommendations, reports, and diagnostic or evaluative statements, including forensic testimony, discussion of any limitations on the data obtained. (See also Standards 2.05, Delegation of Work to Others; 4.01, Maintaining Confidentiality; 9.01, Bases for Assessments; 9.06, Interpreting Assessment Results; and 9.07, Assessment by Unqualified Persons.)

Essential Elements

Psychologists do not commence an assessment without first making sure that the client understands the basic nature, purpose, potential uses of, and techniques involved in the intended assessment process. As is the case for other psychological services (see Standard 3.10, Informed Consent), clients have a right to know in advance what the assessment will entail, any costs involved, who will have access to the results, and how the results might ultimately be used. Effective informed consent requires an explanation of testing in language the client can understand and the opportunity for the client to ask questions. Psychologists ensure that clients or their legal guardians have the capacity to give appropriate informed consent for assessment. When others are employed to administer, score, or interpret test results, clients are informed of this as well. In some contexts, laws and regulations eliminate the requirement for informed consent for assessment.

Common Dilemmas and Conflicts

- Psychologists pressed for time may fail to ensure that clients actually understand the nature and purpose of an assessment.
- Psychologists may erroneously assume that informed consent for assessment is unnecessary in certain forensic or educational contexts.
- Psychologists unfamiliar with relevant laws and statutes governing assessment with minors may fail to get appropriate informed consent from parents or guardians.

Prevention and Positive Practice

✓ Take sufficient time to explain the assessment process to those you assess and obtain informed consent before beginning the evaluation.
✓ Be particularly clear about the reasons for the assessment, limits to confidentiality, others you employ in the assessment process, and the likely uses of the assessment results.
✓ Translate technical jargon related to tests into language clients can understand.
✓ Be familiar with the laws or governmental regulations that might allow assessment without informed consent; even in these cases, try to help clients fully understand the nature and purpose of the proposed assessment.

9.04 Release of Test Data

(a) The term *test data* refers to raw and scaled scores, client/patient responses to test questions or stimuli, and psychologists' notes and recordings concerning client/patient statements and behavior during an examination. Those portions of test materials that include client/patient responses are included in the definition of *test data*. Pursuant to a client/patient release, psychologists provide test data to the client/patient or other persons identified in the release. Psychologists may refrain from releasing test data to protect a client/patient or others from substantial harm or misuse or misrepresentation of the data or the test, recognizing that in many instances release of confidential information under these circumstances is regulated by law. (See also Standard 9.11, Maintaining Test Security.)

(b) In the absence of a client/patient release, psychologists provide test data only as required by law or court order.

Essential Elements

Psychologists release client test data only when a client signs an appropriate release or when required by law. Test data are defined as including those test materials that contain client responses. To the extent possible, psychologists work to clarify in advance who will have access to assessment results. When an appropriate client release or court order is presented, a psychologist then determines which components of the test data and test materials may be ethically released on the basis of factors such as the potential for harm to the client, misuse of the results by a person unqualified to appropriately interpret the results, and federal copyright laws. Psychologists must be cognizant of local statutes and regulations governing the release of confidential information. Finally, psychologists must balance clients' rights to their test data with the obligation to maintain test security (see Standard 9.11, Maintaining Test Security).

Common Dilemmas and Conflicts

- Psychologists who indiscriminately release all test data merely because a client has signed a release may place clients at risk of harm.
- Psychologists who refuse to release test data without attempting to explain their rationale or collaborate with clients to find an ethical resolution are at risk in this area.

Prevention and Positive Practice

- ✓ Make test feedback an ongoing and collaborative process whenever possible.
- ✓ Clarify in advance who will have access to assessment reports and test data.
- ✓ Avoid releasing raw test data to persons unqualified to interpret them accurately.
- ✓ Respond expeditiously to any valid client release or court order; attempt to provide raw data only to a professional qualified to interpret the results, otherwise summarize the results.
- ✓ Always consider both the client's best interests and your legal obligations to the court, other legal authority, and test publishers.

9.05 Test Construction

Psychologists who develop tests and other assessment techniques use appropriate psychometric procedures and current scientific or professional knowledge for test design, standardization, validation, reduction or elimination of bias, and recommendations for use.

Essential Elements

Psychologists who engage in the development of tests and other assessment techniques must be competent in the area of psychometrics; familiar with current standards in this area; and base their work on appropriate procedures for designing, standardizing, and validating their instruments.

Common Dilemmas and Conflicts

- Psychologists who attempt to develop and disseminate an instrument without the requisite competence or without consulting with a competent colleague place themselves at considerable risk of unethical practice.

- Psychologists who publish tests without conducting appropriate standardization and validation studies may place clients and subjects at risk of harm.

Prevention and Positive Practice

✓ Before developing any assessment instrument, ensure your own competence in the area of test development and consult with an experienced colleague.

✓ Use current approaches to test design and demonstrate efforts to reduce bias or negative outcomes for clients and subjects.

✓ Carefully review the APA's Standards for Educational and Psychological Testing (2000; http://www.apa.org/science/standards.html).

✓ In the manual for your test, include adequate information regarding administration, scoring, norms, necessary qualifications for users, reliability, validity, and appropriate interpretation of results.

9.06 Interpreting Assessment Results

When interpreting assessment results, including automated interpretations, psychologists take into account the purpose of the assessment as well as the various test factors, test-taking abilities, and other characteristics of the person being assessed, such as situational, personal, linguistic, and cultural differences, that might affect psychologists' judgments or reduce the accuracy of their interpretations. They indicate any significant limitations of their interpretations. (See also Standards 2.01b and c, Boundaries of Competence, and 3.01, Unfair Discrimination.)

Essential Elements

When interpreting assessment results psychologists take into account all factors that may impact the appropriate interpretation of the results. These factors should include behavioral observations and individual differences such as physical factors that may impact an individual's functioning, culture, and facility with language. Additionally, psychologists must consider all factors that may impact their own judgment when considering assessment results. All potential limitations to the interpretation of assessment results should be included in an explanation of findings.

Common Dilemmas and Conflicts

- Failure to attend to situational factors and individual differences can easily lead to misinterpretations of assessment results.
- Personal biases and a lack of understanding of factors that may impact assessment results—cultural factors in particular—may result in erroneous interpretations of findings.
- Failure to address factors that impact assessment results may lead others to misinterpret or misuse assessment results, possibly resulting in harm to the individual assessed.

Prevention and Positive Practice

- ✓ Educate yourself about and attend to all factors that might impact how assessment results are interpreted.
- ✓ Always include an analysis of the likely impact of these factors on assessment results in all written reports and interpretations of findings.
- ✓ Specifically address potential limitations of assessment results that result from cultural or contextual factors in all written and verbal presentations of findings.

9.07 Assessment by Unqualified Persons

Psychologists do not promote the use of psychological assessment techniques by unqualified persons, except when such use is conducted for training purposes with appropriate supervision. (See also Standard 2.05, Delegation of Work to Others.)

Essential Elements

Psychologists must delegate the use of psychological assessment techniques only to individuals with appropriate training and competence. Further, they must also ensure that they do not violate state licensure laws when delegating assessment duties to unlicensed individuals. When assessment is done by students and trainees, psychologists must provide adequate training and supervision to ensure their competent and effective use of the assessment techniques.

Common Dilemmas and Conflicts

- Psychologists with busy assessment practices may be tempted to delegate test administration and scoring activities to office staff or other inadequately trained subordinates.
- Psychologists with responsibility for students and trainees may erroneously assume they have the requisite competence for simple assessment tasks and subsequently fail to provide needed training and supervision.

Prevention and Positive Practice

✓ Never delegate assessment activities to office staff or other unqualified personnel.

✓ Always assess each student and trainee's level of competence before delegating assessment activities to him or her, and then provide all needed training and supervision.

✓ Be aware of relevant laws regarding testing assistants and technicians in your jurisdiction so you do not violate your licensure law.

9.08 Obsolete Tests and Outdated Test Results

(a) Psychologists do not base their assessment or intervention decisions or recommendations on data or test results that are outdated for the current purpose.

(b) Psychologists do not base such decisions or recommendations on tests and measures that are obsolete and not useful for the current purpose.

Essential Elements

Although the use of psychological tests is of great value in conducting evaluations, psychologists must be sensitive to the gravity of the decisions that are made on the basis of assessment results. Accordingly, psychologists should only use assessments that are reflective of an individual's current functioning unless they are being used in comparison with more current findings to highlight changes in functioning over time. Psychologists should only use the most current version of a test unless an appropriate clinical justification exists for using an older version of a test. Also, psychological tests should be used only for their intended purposes as demonstrated by research showing their reliability and validity.

Common Dilemmas and Conflicts

- Because of the significant expense of some tests, it may be tempting to use older versions of tests to save money even when they are no longer valid for their intended purposes.
- Relying on outdated test results or suggesting that they reflect current functioning may indicate a significant error in judgment.
- Psychologists who fail to become familiar with a test's technical manual may erroneously assume that a test is valid for a certain purpose when it is not.

Prevention and Positive Practice

- ✓ Always make assessment decisions and recommendations based on data that reflect a client's current functioning.
- ✓ Unless a valid reason is present always use the most current version of a psychological test.
- ✓ Never use a test for a purpose that is not supported by empirical data.

9.09 Test Scoring and Interpretation Services

(a) Psychologists who offer assessment or scoring services to other professionals accurately describe the purpose, norms, validity, reliability, and applications of the procedures and any special qualifications applicable to their use.

(b) Psychologists select scoring and interpretation services (including automated services) on the basis of evidence of the validity of the program and procedures as well as on other appropriate considerations. (See also Standard 2.01b and c, Boundaries of Competence.)

(c) **Psychologists retain responsibility for the appropriate application, interpretation, and use of assessment instruments, whether they score and interpret such tests themselves or use automated or other services.**

Essential Elements

The use of technology in psychological assessment can greatly enhance the quality, economy, effectiveness, and ease of assessment services. Automation may greatly enhance the test administration and scoring services psychologists provide. But for interpretation psychologists must exercise caution and accept full responsibility for all interpretive statements made. Allowing automated interpretations of assessment results to supersede psychologists' clinical judgment may result in significant errors and even harm. Those who develop or offer automated assessment services to others must clearly state their purpose, norms, validity, reliability, and appropriate applications to ensure that they are not misused. These same factors must be considered by psychologists before selecting these services.

Common Dilemmas and Conflicts

- Psychologists may be enticed by the ease and convenience of automated assessment services and fail to fully consider their relevance and appropriateness in individual cases or for specific purposes.
- Psychologists may rely on automated interpretations and fail to use their own clinical judgment to the detriment of those they serve.
- Psychologists who develop and offer automated assessment services and who are motivated by fiscal goals may overlook the ethical obligations detailed in this standard.

Prevention and Positive Practice

✓ If you develop or offer automated assessment services, share all information pertinent to making an informed decision relevant to their use.
✓ Only use test scoring and interpretation services after careful consideration of the evidence validating the service with specific populations and specific purposes.

✓ Consider automated interpretations as hypotheses to be considered in light of other relevant information; assessment competence requires a blend of test data and clinical judgment.

9.10 Explaining Assessment Results

Regardless of whether the scoring and interpretation are done by psychologists, by employees or assistants, or by automated or other outside services, psychologists take reasonable steps to ensure that explanations of results are given to the individual or designated representative unless the nature of the relationship precludes provision of an explanation of results (such as in some organizational consulting, preemployment or security screenings, and forensic evaluations), and this fact has been clearly explained to the person being assessed in advance.

Essential Elements

Unless an alternative arrangement was previously agreed upon, psychologists conducting evaluations always provide feedback to those they evaluate, sharing information in a manner that makes the results of the evaluation of relevance and value to that individual. Who will have access to assessment results and to whom feedback will be given should always be clarified and agreed upon up front through the informed consent process with the evaluee.

Common Dilemmas and Conflicts

- It is easy to assume that individuals being evaluated understand who will have access to assessment results and to whom the results will be explained.
- Psychologists conducting evaluations of individuals at the request of third parties may erroneously assume that the individual being evaluated will have access to the assessment results.
- Psychologists who delegate assessment tasks to subordinates may falsely assume that these subordinates understand this standard and that each individual's rights are respected.
- Busy psychologists may fail to take adequate time to explain results sufficiently.

Prevention and Positive Practice

✓ Clarify all expectations regarding feedback and access to assessment results through the informed consent process prior to beginning an evaluation (see Standard 3.10).

✓ Take special care to clarify these expectations when the individual being evaluated is not the one who contracted for the service.

✓ Always ensure that employees, supervisees, and subordinates follow this standard.

✓ Ensure that all parties involved in the referral and assessment process have accurate expectations regarding assessment feedback.

9.11 Maintaining Test Security

The term *test materials* refers to manuals, instruments, protocols, and test questions or stimuli and does not include *test data* as defined in Standard 9.04, Release of Test Data. Psychologists make reasonable efforts to maintain the integrity and security of test materials and other assessment techniques consistent with law and contractual obligations, and in a manner that permits adherence to this Ethics Code.

Essential Elements

Test materials are differentiated from test data, which include the scores and results of evaluations. Test materials include record forms, test stimuli, manuals, and the like. These must be protected to ensure the integrity of the tests. Inappropriate release of test materials could compromise the future usefulness and validity of the tests. In these efforts psychologists strive to follow the Ethics Code while attending to legal and contractual obligations. As such, psychologists should not enter into agreements that will require a violation of test security, nor should psychologists allow clients or other unqualified persons to take custody of test materials.

Common Dilemmas and Conflicts

■ Inadequate attention to test security may result in long-term adverse consequences by impacting the validity of standardized tests and the usefulness of assessment results.

- Psychologists interacting with the legal system may feel compelled to release test materials to nonpsychologists.
- When appropriately releasing test data psychologists may erroneously also release test materials.

Prevention and Positive Practice

✓ Be clear on the definition of test materials, and take special precautions to ensure the integrity and security of all test materials.

✓ Do not feel pressured to release test materials just because they are requested in a legal forum.

✓ Develop ongoing practices and habits that will help ensure the maintenance of test security.

✓ Ensure that office personnel, employees, and supervisees are equally vigilant to test security maintenance.

Standard 10. Therapy

10.01 Informed Consent to Therapy

(a) When obtaining informed consent to therapy as required in Standard 3.10, Informed Consent, psychologists inform clients/patients as early as is feasible in the therapeutic relationship about the nature and anticipated course of therapy, fees, involvement of third parties, and limits of confidentiality and provide sufficient opportunity for the client/patient to ask questions and receive answers. (See also Standards 4.02, Discussing the Limits of Confidentiality, and 6.04, Fees and Financial Arrangements.)

(b) When obtaining informed consent for treatment for which generally recognized techniques and procedures have not been established, psychologists inform their clients/patients of the developing nature of the treatment, the potential risks involved, alternative treatments that may be available, and the voluntary nature of their participation. (See also Standards 2.01e, Boundaries of Competence, and 3.10, Informed Consent.)

(c) When the therapist is a trainee and the legal responsibility for the treatment provided resides with the supervisor, the client/patient, as part of the informed consent procedure, is informed that the therapist is

> in training and is being supervised and is given the name of the supervisor.

Essential Elements

Standard 3.10 of the Ethics Code clearly outlines the obligations of psychologists to carefully inform prospective consumers about the nature of their services so that consumers can make a free and informed decision about participation. Standard 10.01 amplifies this obligation in the context of providing counseling and psychotherapy. As early as possible in any professional relationship—preferably at the outset of the first session—psychologists inform clients orally or in writing and through collaborative conversation about the nature of the psychotherapy relationship. Psychologists provide informed consent using language that clients can understand with ample opportunity for clients to ask clarifying questions. Psychologists carefully document the informed consent process. Key elements of informed consent in psychotherapy include the nature of services and expected treatment outcomes, available alternatives and their relative risks and benefits, fees, billing policies, insurance matters, limits to confidentiality, emergency contact procedures, use of consultation, the likelihood of discomfort or other negative outcomes, and the right to refuse any element of treatment. When psychotherapy procedures or techniques lack sufficient evidence of efficacy—perhaps because the disorder or modality is relatively rare or novel—psychologists should take special care to inform clients about these limitations, potential risks, and reasonable alternatives. Finally, any trainee practicing under the supervision of another professional must explicitly inform clients of the supervisor's name and the nature of the supervision.

Common Dilemmas and Conflicts

- Psychologists who assume that informed consent is an event rather than a process are in danger of offering inadequate informed consent.
- Psychologists with hierarchical or paternalistic attitudes toward clients may presume to know what is best and thereby fail to offer detailed informed consent for psychotherapy.

■ When offering a novel or atypical approach to treatment, psychologists may fail to recognize that the demands for detailed informed consent increase.

Prevention and Positive Practice

✓ Affirm your clients' right to freedom of choice, dignity, and autonomy (Principle E) through careful and detailed informed consent to psychotherapy.

✓ Remember that genuine informed consent can only occur when a client fully understands all the key elements of the treatment to be provided.

✓ Make informed consent an ongoing collaborative process, and welcome clients' participation in reaching consensus about goals and approaches to treatment.

✓ When relevant, clearly communicate to clients your trainee or student status, and make sure clients know who your supervisor is.

10.02 Therapy Involving Couples or Families

(a) When psychologists agree to provide services to several persons who have a relationship (such as spouses, significant others, or parents and children), they take reasonable steps to clarify at the outset (1) which of the individuals are clients/patients and (2) the relationship the psychologist will have with each person. This clarification includes the psychologist's role and the probable uses of the services provided or the information obtained. (See also Standard 4.02, Discussing the Limits of Confidentiality.)

(b) If it becomes apparent that psychologists may be called on to perform potentially conflicting roles (such as family therapist and then witness for one party in divorce proceedings), psychologists take reasonable steps to clarify and modify, or withdraw from, roles appropriately. (See also Standard 3.05c, Multiple Relationships.)

Essential Elements

Psychotherapy for couples and families demands specific competence (see Standard 2). Psychologists with established competence in this area must be especially thorough when providing informed consent (see Standards 3.10 and 10.01) and setting the ground rules for the treatment. Although it is not always easy, psychologists providing psychotherapy to couples and families must clarify which persons are clients, specify the nature of the relationship they will have with each person, and attempt to promote the best interests of all parties involved. Psychologists doing couples and family psychotherapy must also protect the confidentiality of all parties involved unless participants waive this right. Psychologists must be vigilant to the dangers of conflicting roles—especially when conducting concurrent individual and couples or family psychotherapy (see Standard 3.05). When conflicting roles become problematic, psychologists find a thoughtful solution that minimizes harm to all treatment participants.

Common Dilemmas and Conflicts

- Psychologists who fail to consider conflicts of interest and potentially harmful multiple relationships at the outset may create ethical problems in couples and family psychotherapy.
- Although it may be clinically indicated at times, conducting concurrent individual and couples or family psychotherapy heightens the risk of confusion, confidentiality breeches, and conflicting roles.

Prevention and Positive Practice

- ✓ Before providing couples or family psychotherapy, be sure that you are competent by virtue of education, training, and supervised experience.
- ✓ Provide detailed and thorough informed consent both at the outset of psychotherapy and as couples or family psychotherapy progresses so that all involved have a clear understanding of expected roles, allegiances, and limits to confidentiality.
- ✓ Work to prevent your personal beliefs and biases (e.g., concerning marriage, family structure, couples roles) from constraining client autonomy or choice.
- ✓ Be vigilant to conflicts between the best interests of individuals and a couple or family, and work to clarify and resolve these conflicts while minimizing harm.

✓ Seek consultation and be open with your clients if it becomes unclear whether continued psychotherapy is likely to be appropriate or helpful or if potentially conflicting roles emerge.

10.03 Group Therapy

When psychologists provide services to several persons in a group setting, they describe at the outset the roles and responsibilities of all parties and the limits of confidentiality.

Essential Elements

Before offering group therapy, psychologists ensure they are competent in this area (see Standard 2) and provide clear informed consent to all group participants. Essential elements of informed consent to group therapy include the specific purpose of the group, expectations for group members, rules and limitations regarding confidentiality, likely benefits and potential risks of psychotherapy, and the right to decline participation. Psychologists should inform clients in advance if strong emotional expression is likely, and they must make every effort to protect clients from harm (see Standard 3.04) resulting from either the group process or the actions of other members.

Common Dilemmas and Conflicts

- Psychologists who, because of theoretical or other biases, believe that all clients can and should benefit from groups may coerce participation in clients who are unlikely to benefit from or do not wish to have group psychotherapy.
- Although clinically indicated at times, providing concurrent individual and group psychotherapy raises the risk of financial exploitation of clients who may not require both modalities.
- Because group process is less predictable than individual psychotherapy, group psychotherapy may place the client at slightly higher risk of negative therapeutic outcomes or violations of confidentiality by group members.
- It may be difficult to simultaneously serve the best interests of each group member.

Prevention and Positive Practice

✓ Ensure your competence to practice group psychotherapy before working in this area.

✓ Be familiar with guidelines and standards bearing on group psychotherapy.

✓ Thoroughly orient each client to group process, and provide careful informed consent for the group; when possible, do this prior to the first group session.

✓ Convey an expectation that group members will honor confidentiality while informing members that this aspiration cannot be guaranteed.

✓ Recognize that not all clients will benefit from group psychotherapy; select group members thoughtfully.

10.04 Providing Therapy to Those Served by Others

In deciding whether to offer or provide services to those already receiving mental health services elsewhere, psychologists carefully consider the treatment issues and the potential client's/patient's welfare. Psychologists discuss these issues with the client/patient or another legally authorized person on behalf of the client/patient in order to minimize the risk of confusion and conflict, consult with the other service providers when appropriate, and proceed with caution and sensitivity to the therapeutic issues.

Essential Elements

When persons who are currently receiving services from other professionals approach psychologists and request services, psychologists must be especially careful to balance several important considerations. These include the circumstances and welfare of the person soliciting services, psychologists' obligation to treat other professionals with respect, and any unique therapeutic issues such as abuse or exploitation by another provider. It is always important to have a clear and transparent discussion with prospective clients about the problems inherent in providing services to those served by others. When the prospective client agrees and circumstances allow, it is preferable for the psychologist to discuss his or her role with the client's other service providers as a way of reducing the risk of conflict or misunderstanding. As a general rule, it is not appropriate to make uninvited solicitation of those psychologists know are served by other providers.

Common Dilemmas and Conflicts

- Psychologists who are struggling financially may be more prone to inappropriately solicit clients served by other providers.
- At times, persons with personality impairment may attempt to engage multiple professionals simultaneously, thereby creating conflict between professionals.
- Accepting new clients without inquiring about concurrent services or failing to respond with caution when concurrent services are revealed places psychologists at risk in this area.
- Failing to clarify roles and boundaries with a client served by another provider increases the risk of negative treatment outcomes.
- When a client has been harmed or exploited by another provider, it may be tempting to file a complaint or confront the provider without the client's permission. This would violate confidentiality.

Prevention and Positive Practice

- ✓ Avoid uninvited solicitation of those served by other professionals.
- ✓ Proceed cautiously when a person served by another professional seeks treatment, and clearly express your concern about the potential for conflict.
- ✓ Seek permission to discuss the request with the person's other provider if this is appropriate.
- ✓ Be sensitive to the possibility that a person served by another provider has been harmed or exploited by that provider. In this case, it is appropriate to provide treatment without contacting the other provider.

10.05 Sexual Intimacies With Current Therapy Clients/Patients

Psychologists do not engage in sexual intimacies with current therapy clients/patients.

Essential Elements

It is never appropriate to engage in sexual intimacies with a current client. Clients depend on psychologists to only take actions that promote their best interests. As a result of the nature of the professional relationship, psychologists' relative power vis-à-vis clients, clients' vulnerability, clients' trust of psychologists, and the inevitable harm that results from sexually intimate relationships between client and psychologist, it is simply never appropriate to have sexual contact of any kind with current clients.

Common Dilemmas and Conflicts

- Psychologists experiencing personal distress or relationship problems may blur boundaries and seek emotional support and physical comfort from clients.
- Those who do not actively address—through supervision or consultation—feelings of attraction to clients may be at risk of acting on them.
- Psychologists who treat individuals with histories of abuse, personality disturbance, or difficulty abiding by boundary limits may face special challenges in attempting to help these clients while avoiding boundary violations.

Prevention and Positive Practice

- ✓ Actively address your emotional needs, urges, impulses, and feelings toward clients through ongoing supervision and personal psychotherapy.
- ✓ Engage in ongoing self-care to ensure that personal needs and issues do not spill over into the psychotherapy relationship.
- ✓ Accept that it is never appropriate to engage in a sexually intimate relationship with any client, no matter what the circumstances.

✓ If you are even entertaining the possibility of a romantic or sexual relationship with a client, seek immediate consultation from a trusted and competent colleague.

✓ Soberly consider the devastating impact of sexual involvement with a client on the client, on the public's perception of your profession, and on your career.

10.06 Sexual Intimacies With Relatives or Significant Others of Current Therapy Clients/Patients

Psychologists do not engage in sexual intimacies with individuals they know to be close relatives, guardians, or significant others of current clients/patients. Psychologists do not terminate therapy to circumvent this standard.

Essential Elements

Just as sexually intimate relationships with clients (see Standard 10.05) are inappropriate, sexual relationships with those closely associated with clients, such as the parent of a child patient, are also not appropriate. Such intimate relationships often lead to impaired objectivity and judgment on psychologists' part and frequently result in exploitation or harm to clients. Additionally, psychologists should never terminate psychotherapy to enter into an intimate relationship with such individuals. All treatment decisions should be motivated by the client's treatment needs, not psychologists' personal interests or romantic goals.

Common Dilemmas and Conflicts

- Forming close alliances with clients' family members and significant others can heighten the risk of more intimate relationships.
- Sexual intimacy with a client's relatives or significant others often diminishes the value of treatment and creates confusion and discomfort for clients.
- Psychologists who develop romantic or sexual feelings for clients' family members or significant others may be tempted to terminate treatment to pursue these other relationships.

Prevention and Positive Practice

✓ Always consider your obligations to clients to include all those closely related to or associated with them.

✓ Never engage in actions that will jeopardize a client's trust in you.

✓ Treatment termination should never be motivated by your personal needs.

10.07 Therapy With Former Sexual Partners

Psychologists do not accept as therapy clients/patients persons with whom they have engaged in sexual intimacies.

Essential Elements

Psychologists aspire to neutrality and objectivity in their professional relationships and ensure that treatment decisions are motivated by clients' best interests. Having previously engaged in a sexually intimate relationship with an individual seriously diminishes the psychologist's ability to achieve the objectivity needed for a successful psychotherapy relationship.

Common Dilemmas and Conflicts

■ As a result of familiarity with a former lover's issues and needs, a psychologist may feel uniquely qualified to provide professional services.

■ Ongoing feelings of care or concern may make it difficult to refuse a treatment request from an individual with whom one has previously engaged in sexual intimacies.

■ Psychologists who downplay or ignore the lingering power of romantic and emotional bonds with former lovers may be at risk in this area.

Prevention and Positive Practice

✓ Focus on your former lover's best interests and your inability to provide genuinely objective treatment.

✓ Refer all former sexual or romantic partners to competent colleagues for any needed treatment; frame the referral as an act of genuine care versus rejection.

✓ Seek collegial consultation if you find yourself rationalizing why it may be acceptable to provide treatment to a former lover.

10.08 Sexual Intimacies With Former Therapy Clients/Patients

(a) Psychologists do not engage in sexual intimacies with former clients/patients for at least two years after cessation or termination of therapy.

(b) Psychologists do not engage in sexual intimacies with former clients/patients even after a two-year interval except in the most unusual circumstances. Psychologists who engage in such activity after the two years following cessation or termination of therapy and of having no sexual contact with the former client/patient bear the burden of demonstrating that there has been no exploitation, in light of all relevant factors, including (1) the amount of time that has passed since therapy terminated; (2) the nature, duration, and intensity of the therapy; (3) the circumstances of termination; (4) the client's/patient's personal history; (5) the client's/patient's current mental status; (6) the likelihood of adverse impact on the client/patient; and (7) any statements or actions made by the therapist during the course of therapy suggesting or inviting the possibility of a posttermination sexual or romantic relationship with the client/patient. (See also Standard 3.05, Multiple Relationships.)

Essential Elements

It is generally unacceptable to enter into sexually intimate relationships with former clients. Because of the likelihood of client harm and exploitation, sexual intimacies with former clients may only be appropriate under the most unusual circumstances. To engage in such relationships one must have had no intimate contact with the former client for at least 2 years after treatment termination and then only after meeting seven specific criteria intended to ensure that former clients are not exploited or harmed. If unsure of how to apply these seven criteria, one should consult with an experienced colleague prior to engaging in the sexually intimate relationship.

Common Dilemmas and Conflicts

- Psychologists who believe that they can act with a client's best interests in mind when feeling strong sexual attraction and planning a future romantic relationship with the client are prone to poor judgment and may cause harm to the client.
- Assuming that a former client's dependence and vulnerability to exploitation are no longer present simply because 2 years have passed since treatment ended heightens risk of harm.
- Psychologists who terminate treatment prematurely for the purpose of starting the 2-year moratorium are acting unethically.

Prevention and Positive Practice

- ✓ Avoid all romantic and sexual involvements with former clients.
- ✓ Seek professional consultation, clinical supervision, and possibly personal psychotherapy if you begin entertaining plans to begin such involvement with a former client.
- ✓ Consider each client's mental health issues and needs when making decisions about relationships with former clients.
- ✓ Consider the potential impact of such involvement on the public's view of psychologists and psychotherapy in general.
- ✓ Always focus on clients' best interests and needs from the perspective of their psychologist, not a potential lover.

10.09 Interruption of Therapy

When entering into employment or contractual relationships, psychologists make reasonable efforts to provide for orderly and appropriate resolution of responsibility for client/patient care in the event that the employment or contractual relationship ends, with paramount consid-

eration given to the welfare of the client/patient. (See also
Standard 3.12, Interruption of Psychological Services.)

Essential Elements

Because all employment and contractual relationships may end
at some time, it is best to make arrangements from the outset
regarding who will take over the care of a psychologist's clients
should his or her position be terminated. Making such arrangements in advance will help ensure that each client's treatment
needs are addressed and that continuity of care will occur.

Common Dilemmas and Conflicts

- When psychologists erroneously assume that they can
  continue treating clients elsewhere should their position
  or contract be terminated, legal battles ensue and client
  care may suffer.
- Assuming that transition arrangements can be worked out
  informally if and when employment ends may have adverse
  consequences for clients.

Prevention and Positive Practice

- ✓ Always make arrangements in writing from the outset to
  ensure that clients' treatment needs will be addressed in a
  timely manner.
- ✓ Ensure that such written agreements specify how referrals
  and transitions to other care providers will be carried out.
- ✓ Make planning for potential interruption of services part
  of the ongoing process of informed consent (see Standards
  3.10 and 10.01).

10.10 Terminating Therapy

(a) Psychologists terminate therapy when it becomes
reasonably clear that the client/patient no longer
needs the service, is not likely to benefit, or is being
harmed by continued service.

(b) Psychologists may terminate therapy when threatened or otherwise endangered by the client/patient
or another person with whom the client/patient has
a relationship.

(c) **Except where precluded by the actions of clients/patients or third-party payors, prior to termination psychologists provide pretermination counseling and suggest alternative service providers as appropriate.**

Essential Elements

The process of termination is an important one; it must be addressed in a manner consistent with the client's best interests. Over the course of treatment if it becomes, or should become, clear to psychologists that a client is not benefiting from treatment and there is no significant likelihood that he or she will benefit from ongoing treatment, they should terminate the professional relationship. In this situation, and whenever possible, they should provide pretermination counseling and offer referral suggestions for those in need of ongoing services. If a client or a person associated with the client threatens the psychologist, treatment may immediately be terminated without any pretermination counseling.

Common Dilemmas and Conflicts

- Psychologists who are struggling financially may overlook the client's best interests by continuing treatment when it is not benefiting the client.
- Assuming that clients do not need pretermination counseling and failing to make referrals for those still in need of treatment can cause harm to them.
- Strong feelings about a client (e.g., anger, fear, sexual attraction) may lead to ineffective, incomplete, or harmful termination of treatment.

Prevention and Positive Practice

- ✓ Always describe the process of termination in informed consent and consider termination an essential phase of each client's treatment.
- ✓ Focus on each client's treatment needs and make appropriate referrals when it is reasonably clear that the client will not benefit from further treatment with you.
- ✓ Seek consultation before abruptly terminating a client's treatment, such as in the case of a threatening or dangerous client.

PART II

DECISION MAKING AND ETHICAL PRACTICE IN SPECIFIC AREAS

At times, psychologists face ethical quandaries, professional crises, and ethical–legal conflicts. A suicidal client, a mandatory reporting situation, or an ethics complaint can easily generate stress and anxiety and diminish decision-making. In Part II of the *Ethics Desk Reference for Psychologists* (EDR) we offer concise and accessible guidance for these and other situations. We begin with a clear-cut ethical-decision-making model. When an ethical quandary arises, we recommend slowing down the process and deliberately working through each step in the model. By doing so, psychologists increase the probability of asking the right questions, considering relevant variables, and getting the right consultation before proceeding.

In Part II we also offer concise guidance for working with managed care organizations, offering clinical supervision and collegial consultation, effectively responding to suicidal clients, complying with mandatory reporting requirements, and effectively preparing for and handling client terminations, areas that tend to be most challenging for psychologists. This portion of the EDR ends with pertinent advice for responding effectively to an ethics complaint or malpractice suit. An appendix then provides key ethics resources for psychologists that include professional guidelines, ethics publications and resources, key psychology organizations, American Psychological Association (APA) practice guidelines, licensing board contacts, and resources for continuing education in ethics.

Although the guidance in Part II is designed to help psychologists cut right to the key processes and considerations when practicing in specific areas or circumstances, nothing in this section should be construed as an ethical mandate. None of these recommendations are enforceable under the APA Ethics Code. These strategies and recommendations are designed merely to augment the Code and enable more effective decision making and professional practice.

Making an Ethical Decision: A Process Model

Sound ethical decisions hinge on a sound decision-making process. When ethical quandaries arise—especially when they arise suddenly—it is easy to feel daunted, even overwhelmed. Psychologists will be well served by using a clear approach to facing ethical dilemmas. Deliberate use of a decision-making process helps psychologists to slow down, calm down, gather their thoughts, and ensure that they have considered all relevant variables, the interests of all those impacted by their decisions, and the wisdom of colleagues with whom they might consult.

Whether making a preventative policy decision or handling a professional crisis, the following decision-making model should help psychologists to slow things down, consider important ethical obligations, and act with the best interests of those they serve at the fore. We present this model as a process with 10 important stages. Consultation appears twice by design; good consultation is often essential to making a wise ethical decision. Psychologists should recognize that these stages are not purely linear; it is often useful to return to an earlier stage in the process as new wrinkles arise, good consultation occurs, or as psychologists feel the need to rethink their conclusions at an earlier stage.

Stage 1: Define the Situation Clearly

✓ Articulate the exact nature of the situation.
✓ Gather as many relevant facts and details as possible.
✓ Pinpoint the primary quandary or conflict(s).

✓ Begin to consider the potential ethical issues and your obligations.

Stage 2: Determine Who Will Be Impacted

✓ Identify the primary client as well as any secondary clients.
✓ Consider the full range of persons who might be impacted by your decision.
✓ Articulate your professional obligations to and the rights of each person and group involved.
✓ Be especially sensitive to the potential for harm to any person involved.
✓ Reflect on your obligation to promote the best interests of those involved.
✓ Begin to consider the potential impact of various decisions on those involved.

Stage 3: Refer to the Ethical Principles and Standards

✓ Review the American Psychological Association (APA) Ethics Code.
✓ Identify the standards and general principles most germane to your situation.
✓ When specific standards are ambiguous regarding your question, consider the more fundamental obligations conveyed in the general ethical principles.
✓ Consider consulting one or more current ethics texts or articles on ethics in professional journals for additional guidance or case examples.
✓ Use the Ethics Code to eliminate clearly unethical responses.

Stage 4: Refer to Relevant Laws, Regulations, and Professional Guidelines

✓ Review legal statutes and regulations bearing on psychology in your jurisdiction.
✓ Consider agency and institutional policies.
✓ Identify and review any relevant practice guidelines bearing on the situation, client type, problem, and type of service.

✓ Consult with a lawyer to determine your legal obligations and the legal consequences of various courses of action.

✓ Consult with colleagues or ethics organizations concerning potential conflicts between ethical and legal obligations.

Stage 5: Reflect Honestly on Personal Feelings and Competence

✓ Take time to reflect honestly about the thoughts and feelings aroused by the situation.

✓ Consider whether feelings aroused about yourself (e.g., shame, diminished esteem) or others involved (e.g., anger, anxiety, sexual attraction) may negatively impact your decision making.

✓ Honestly consider whether you have the requisite competence—defined by education, training, and supervised experience—to handle the situation effectively.

Stage 6: Consult With Trusted Colleagues

✓ Carefully select one or more colleagues whom you know to have experience in the area of concern, good judgment, and solid familiarity with ethical and legal issues.

✓ Seek consultant referrals, if needed, from local or national psychology organizations.

✓ Select consultants who are honest, forthright, and respectful of confidentiality.

✓ Prepare carefully for the consultation by summarizing key facts, apparent ethical issues, personal concerns, and possible courses of action.

Stage 7: Formulate Alternative Courses of Action

✓ Take time to think about the full range of possible responses to the situation.

✓ Consider all of the ways you might proceed in light of the facts at hand (e.g., full array of interventions, research designs, methods of confronting a student or colleague).

✓ Consider the feasibility and ethical and legal implications of each approach.

Stage 8: Consider Possible Outcomes for All Parties Involved

- ✓ Evaluate the probable impact for each client and stakeholder of each course of action considered.
- ✓ Enumerate possible outcomes for those involved, paying particular attention to potential risks and benefits.
- ✓ Assess the implications of each approach in light of your ethical and legal obligations.
- ✓ Document this reasoning process.

Stage 9: Consult With Colleagues and Ethics Committees

- ✓ Consult with a respected colleague once more—particularly if the best plan of action has not emerged by this point.
- ✓ Seek confirmation that your plan makes the most sense ethically, legally, and professionally.

Stage 10: Make a Decision, Monitor the Outcome, and Modify Your Plan as Needed

- ✓ On the basis of the first nine stages and all relevant information available to you at this time, select the best option and implement it.
- ✓ When possible, discuss your decision and your rationale with stakeholders.
- ✓ Always take full responsibility for the decision.
- ✓ Carefully monitor—to the extent possible—the effects of your course of action on those involved. Modify your plan as needed, and continue this process until the best possible outcomes are achieved.
- ✓ Clearly document each stage of your ethical-decision-making process.

Managed Care

The use of insurance to cover health care expenses is a widely accepted practice in our society. Many health insurance policies provide some coverage for mental health treatment. Managed care is a cost containment system used by insurance companies to limit expenses by reducing what they view as inappropriate use of services. This may involve utilization review procedures, fee reductions for health professionals, and controlling consumers' access to care. Psychologists who participate in managed care plans typically do so in the hope of receiving referrals from the insurance plan. In some geographic areas it may be difficult for psychologists not to participate in managed care plans because of their large market share. This may be especially true for psychologists who are new to an area or who are just beginning their careers.

Participation in managed care brings with it a number of ethical dilemmas and challenges for psychologists. Careful attention to these ethical issues prior to signing a contract to participate is essential. Particularly relevant ethics issues include informed consent, competence, confidentiality, fees and financial arrangements, conflicts of interest, advocacy for clients, documentation, termination, and abandonment, among others. Psychologists must understand that a managed care contract is a legally binding document. It is important to consult with an attorney before signing any contract; these contracts may bring obligations and risks that are not always readily apparent.

Key Recommendations

✓ It may be helpful to have contracts reviewed by an attorney prior to agreeing to participate with any managed care plan. Clarify your obligations under the contract such as requirements for how quickly clients must be seen.

✓ Be sure you have the needed competence to work effectively with specific managed care organizations (MCOs). For instance, some require a brief treatment or group treatment approach. Psychologists without competence in these approaches should not participate with these plans.

✓ It is wise to confirm clients' insurance benefits prior to providing treatment so that each party has realistic expectations of the type and extent of services funded by the insurer. This also helps prevent abandonment of clients should benefits expire while treatment is ongoing.

✓ Be aware of the services allowed and disallowed by the client's policy. For example, many MCOs do not provide coverage for psychological testing or marital counseling.

✓ Assess each client's treatment needs at the outset, and agree on a treatment plan that is realistic on the basis of the coverage provided by the insurer.

✓ Include any restrictions or limitations on treatment from the MCO in the informed consent agreement. Ensure that clients understand their financial responsibilities and those of the MCO.

✓ Be aware of each MCO's utilization review requirements from the outset, and always complete this process before required deadlines.

✓ When it is your clinical assessment that a client requires ongoing treatment, but an MCO renders an adverse utilization review decision denying further services (assuming benefits are not exhausted for that year), it is essential to appeal or have the client appeal this adverse decision.

✓ Remember that MCOs cannot prevent you from providing treatment; they can only withhold payment for services they regard as unnecessary. Never let an MCO's fiscally motivated decisions supersede your clinical treatment decisions. Offer to continue providing needed treatment while awaiting the outcome of an appeal.

✓ If an appeal is denied, consider pursuing other means of advocacy on your client's behalf such as through the Grievance Office of your state's Attorney General's Office, the state Insurance Commissioner's Office, or other similar agency.

✓ Be wary of conflicts of interest that may influence your clinical decision making. For instance, if you are concerned that an MCO will drop you from its panel because of use patterns, you may be tempted to provide clients with less care than is clinically indicated.

✓ Never change a client's diagnosis or provide fraudulent information in the hope of obtaining additional treatment authorizations (e.g., listing a more serious diagnosis or a lower Global Assessment of Functioning score); never mis-identify the client on insurance paperwork (e.g., listing an individual when a couple is being treated, listing other family members); and never provide one service when billing for another (many MCOs will authorize many psychotherapy sessions but no testing sessions).

✓ Be sure clients understand the possible impact on their privacy if they use their insurance benefits. Psychologists have no control over clinical information once it is submitted to the MCO.

✓ Always document services with an eye toward meeting the MCO's utilization review standards and professional guidelines bearing on clinical documentation. Take care to provide the minimum information needed to meet this standard in order to safeguard privacy. Document all contacts with MCO personnel, and keep copies of all utilization review materials.

✓ If you find yourself resentful of managed care restrictions, requirements, and reimbursement rates, be cognizant of the impact of your feelings on clinical effectiveness and treatment of clients. Consider terminating managed care contracts and seeking other practice options.

✓ When terminating managed care contracts, follow contract provisions for advanced notice, and be sure to fully address each client's treatment needs either personally or through appropriate referrals to competent professionals in their insurance network.

See Standards 1.03, 3.04, 3.06, 3.10–3.12, 4.01–4.06, 6.01, 6.04, 6.06, 6.07, 9.02, 10.01, 10.09, and 10.10.

Clinical Supervision and Consultation

Clinical supervision and consultation are essential elements of psychologists' professional development and a frequent domain of practice for many psychologists. Supervision is pervasive from the first graduate school placement through periodic expansions in psychologists' areas of expertise; seeking consultation from a skilled and experienced colleague is also a hallmark of professional wisdom and positive prevention. No psychologist can be expert in all areas or have all the answers in dealing with challenging clients. The active use of consultation throughout psychologists' careers is an important ethical imperative. Consultation helps ensure that psychologists remain competent, that clients receive the best possible service, that psychologists' clinical judgment is in line with the thinking of experienced colleagues, and that psychologists have not overlooked critical ethical or legal imperatives. Those who provide supervision or consultation should ensure that they are competent both in the clinical area they are supervising and in the practice of supervision as well. Supervisors and consultants must see themselves as professional role models whose behavior will likely be emulated by supervisees and consultees. Additionally, the nature and quality of the supervision and consultation provided will likely have a significant impact on the professional development of trainees and colleagues and on the treatment provided to their clients, both at present and in the future. Psychologists serving as supervisors and consultants must therefore be cognizant of the significant professional responsibility they bear and act accordingly. The checklist that follows offers specific recommendations that should help both supervisors and supervisees to meet these obligations.

Key Recommendations

✓ Use consultation at various times throughout your career. It is not just for trainees and graduate students.

✓ From the outset, use an informed consent agreement between supervisors and supervisees to ensure that all expectations (such as meeting times, fees, responsibilities, emergency contact information, and evaluations if any) are clarified and agreed to up front.

✓ Integrate relevant ethics and legal issues into all aspects of supervision and consultation.

✓ Attend to relevant diversity issues both in the supervision and consultation dyad and in the supervisee's and consultee's clinical work.

✓ Differentiate supervision from consultation. Although it may vary by jurisdiction, supervisors typically accept full responsibility for the clinical work of the supervisee. Clarify this in the informed consent agreement.

✓ Carefully assess each supervisee's level of competence and requisite training needs from the outset. The type and intensity of supervision should match the supervisee's training needs.

✓ Provide adequate oversight of supervisees, and only delegate those tasks and activities supervisees are competent to perform.

✓ Attend to laws and regulations relevant to students and trainees such as required hours of supervision and requirements for one-on-one and in-person periodic evaluations. Ensure trainees use only those titles allowed by law and that they do not misrepresent themselves.

✓ Ensure that all clients both understand and sign an informed consent agreement to have the supervisee's work supervised. Address issues of confidentiality here.

✓ When expanding your competence into new areas of practice, ensure adequate didactic training and consultation. Provide new services independently only after a joint decision to this effect is made with the consultant.

✓ It is essential for supervisors and consultants and recommended for supervisees that documentation of these sessions be maintained. This provides a tangible record of what transpired as well as a plan for follow-up action; good documentation is the standard of practice for supervisors and consultants and helps to minimize misunderstandings.

✓ Provide supervisees with regular feedback, verbally and in writing, and provide opportunities to remediate any deficiencies.

✓ Model appropriate boundaries in the supervisory relationship, and be sure to address with supervisees issues such as their reactions to and feelings toward clients, the appropriate crossing of boundaries, and the need to avoid boundary violations (careful attention to cultural differences here is essential).

See Standards 2.01, 3.11, 4.02, 6.01, 7.01–7.07

Suicidal Clients

Few events elicit as many powerful emotions in psychologists as a client's suicide attempt or completion. When a client is seriously depressed, abusing substances, or going through painful circumstances, psychologists must be particularly alert to suicide risk. When a client alludes to or admits hopelessness or thoughts of suicide, psychologists must become very active in assessing suicide risk and intervening as necessary to keep their client safe. Because suicidal clients may arouse feelings ranging from anger to anxiety to helplessness, psychologists must be careful not to become punitive or paralyzed in their work with suicidal persons. Principle A (Beneficence and Nonmaleficence) enjoins psychologists to safeguard the welfare of those with whom they work. Helping clients to avoid suicide is clearly congruent with this ethical principle.

When psychologists have concerns about a client's suicide risk, they should remember that there are several known risk factors for suicide. Although none of these factors alone portends suicidal behavior, each factor should be considered, both at the outset of a clinical relationship and periodically as circumstances change or clients become more depressed or impaired. When assessing risk of suicide, psychologists should consider the risk factors listed in the next section.

Suicide Risk Factors

- Sex: Men are four times more likely to complete suicide.
- Age: Elderly people and adolescents are at greater risk.

- Race: Caucasians have the highest rates of suicide.
- Depression: A history of a mood disorder (e.g., depression, bipolar disorder).
- Alcohol: Alcohol abuse or dependence is common.
- History of attempts: Previous attempts predict future attempts.
- Chronic illness: Chronic or serious physical illness or disability.
- Family history: Suicide attempts in family or important friends.
- Impulsivity: A history of impulsive or aggressive behavior.
- Hopelessness: Loss of interest or hope in the future.
- Loss: Serious and recent losses.
- Psychosis: Serious disorganization or other psychotic symptoms.
- Social support: Lack of social support.
- Plan and means: An organized plan and access to means raise the risk.

In addition to these general risk factors, there are several warning signs of suicide that may manifest in a client's behavior prior to a suicide attempt. Again, no single factor predicts a suicide; rather, each factor should raise the psychologist's concern and prompt further inquiry about potential ideation, intent, and planning.

Suicide Warning Signs

- Talking about suicide: Talking or writing about suicide.
- Verbal cues: "I wish I were dead. What's the point?"
- Neglecting self: Decreased focus on hygiene and appearance.
- Worsening mood: Becoming more depressed and hopeless.
- Sudden loss: Client has sudden personal crisis or relational loss.
- Sudden change in mood: Dramatic elevation in mood.
- Suicide planning: Formulating a plan for suicide.
- Withdrawal: Becoming distant and withdrawn from relationships.
- Preparations: Giving away belongings, buying a weapon, saving pills.
- Saying goodbye: Offering vague thanks or goodbye to friends, family members, or psychologist.

In addition to considering the key risk factors and clinical warning signs for suicide, psychologists should also be mindful of the following recommendations. Each is a salient reminder for preventing suicide or responding to a direct suicide threat.

Key Recommendations

✓ When working with high-risk clients, seriously consider consultation with colleagues with demonstrated expertise in this area.

✓ Be certain that risk to self is one of the exceptions to confidentiality clearly articulated in the informed consent agreement.

✓ Be sure that you have adequate training and experience with the assessment and treatment of suicidal behaviors.

✓ Periodically consider suicide risk in all clients. Address suicide risk in initial intakes for every client and thereafter as a client's symptoms and circumstances warrant.

✓ Initiate discussion of suicidal ideation or planning when risk factors or warning signs are present. Be proactive in directly broaching the topic of suicide when you have reasonable concern.

✓ Be familiar with procedures for psychiatric hospitalization in your area.

✓ Be familiar with local and state statutes and policies bearing on involuntary psychiatric admission.

✓ Make sure clients with suicidal ideation know exactly how to reach you or your emergency coverage at all hours of the day.

✓ When a client exhibits risk factors for suicide or is seriously depressed and has suicidal ideation with a plan and intent, seek hospitalization for the client immediately.

✓ Depressed or at-risk clients with ideation but without a plan or intent may be best served by a hospitalization or may be treated on an outpatient basis; consultation with a trusted colleague is advised before making this decision.

✓ Although asking a client to contract—verbally or in writing—that he or she will not harm him- or herself may be helpful, remember that there is no reliable evidence confirming this as an effective intervention.

✓ Clearly document your rationale for diagnostic, suicide risk, and treatment plan decisions in the client's record.

✓ Remember that clients with mood disorders, psychotic disorders, and substance abuse disorders are at greater risk of suicide than other clients; accurate diagnosis and appropriate vigilance are essential.

✓ When supervising, be particularly active and thorough in helping supervisees manage suicidal clients.

✓ Work with the client and family members to reduce access to means for suicide when a client has expressed suicidal ideation or a plan.

✓ Be sensitive to your own feelings about clients' suicidality; if your own feelings (e.g., anger, anxiety) begin to diminish therapeutic effectiveness, seek consultation and consider making an appropriate referral.

✓ If your life has been personally impacted by suicide, ensure that your own loss and resulting feelings do not diminish the effectiveness of your work with suicidal clients.

✓ Whenever possible, avoid transferring or terminating services with an acutely suicidal client.

✓ When referring a client with current or chronic struggles with suicidal ideas, take extra care to ensure that the client initiates treatment with a new provider.

✓ Consider providing suicidal outpatient clients with contact information to the National Suicide Prevention Lifeline (http://www.suicidepreventionlifeline.org) and other suicide hotlines as a backup to your own contact information.

See Standards 2.01, 2.05, 3.04, 4.02, 4.05, and 10.10.

Mandatory Reporting Requirements

The importance of maintaining confidentiality is a hallmark of the psychotherapy relationship. But at times, maintaining confidentiality may not be in a client's best interests. State laws generally recognize certain groups as vulnerable populations, specifically individuals who rely on others for their care and well-being. These groups are accorded special protections under the law. They typically include minors, elderly persons, and developmentally delayed individuals. All states have laws specifying mandatory child abuse, elder abuse, or vulnerable adult reporting requirements. Typically, these laws provide legal definitions of abuse, neglect, exploitation, and related concepts. Most state child abuse reporting laws include physical, emotional, and sexual abuse as well as neglect in their definitions. Elder abuse reporting requirements may include definitions of abuse, neglect, self-neglect, and exploitation.

Psychologists who have a reasonable suspicion of abuse or neglect of a vulnerable person covered by state law must make a mandatory report to the appropriate local agency, typically a department of social services or department of child protective services. Relevant laws will specify whether the report must be made verbally, in writing, or both and when the report(s) must be made. Additionally, these laws typically provide licensed health professionals with immunity from liability if they make such a report in good faith. One does not have to prove that abuse has occurred or is occurring but must have a reasonable suspicion of it.

Key Recommendations

✓ Always include mandatory reporting requirements as exceptions to confidentiality in the informed consent agreement, and ensure that all parties are aware of and understand your obligations under the law.

✓ Study your state's laws; know the definitions of key terms related to abuse and neglect; and be aware of your reporting obligations.

✓ Educate yourself on the signs of abuse and neglect, and always assess for their presence. Ensure competence through ongoing training.

✓ Be cognizant of differences that result from various forms of diversity including race, ethnicity, culture, gender, socioeconomic status, religion, sexual orientation, language, and disability; parenting styles and techniques that are unfamiliar or unusual are not necessarily abusive or harmful.

✓ When the requirement to make a report is present, inform all involved parties of this. Try to include them in the reporting process, and highlight the importance of following through with this obligation.

✓ Never ignore signs of abuse or neglect, and never decide not to make a mandated report because you fear that it will not help or might even make things worse for your client.

✓ Do not conduct your own investigation of suspected or reported abuse or neglect and then decide on your own whether further action is needed. Leave the investigating to those trained and authorized to do so.

✓ Never use a report of suspected abuse or neglect as a punitive action.

✓ Be aware that abuse and neglect fall on a continuum. Not all behavior that you find inappropriate or troubling will meet the legal definitions of abuse and neglect.

✓ If unsure of your obligations in a particular situation, carefully review the law, consult with a knowledgeable colleague, or consult with an attorney or ethics committee.

✓ Document all information that leads you to the decision to file a report, including all consultations, your decision-making process, all actions taken, and any outcomes.

✓ Actively work to integrate the mandatory reporting process into ongoing treatment to achieve the best psychotherapeutic outcomes possible.

✓ When a report is not required by law but clinical concerns still exist, be sure to address these issues in ongoing treatment.

Termination
and Abandonment

From the start of each clinical relationship, psychologists work to achieve a successful ending. Successful termination most often occurs when the agreed-on treatment goals have been achieved, but treatment may end for a wide range of reasons. These include changes in a client's financial or employment situation, loss of insurance coverage, a client's relocation, a client's dissatisfaction with treatment or with the psychologist, or the psychologist's becoming unavailable because of illness, disability, or retirement. In addition, psychologists should terminate a client's treatment when it is or should become clear that the client is not benefiting from treatment, when a potentially harmful multiple relationship begins or is discovered, or when the psychologist no longer has the competence necessary to meet the client's treatment needs. In each of these circumstances, the psychologist must provide pretermination counseling, assess the client's ongoing treatment needs, and make appropriate referrals for ongoing treatment with other competent professionals. The one time termination may occur without providing pretermination counseling and needed referrals is when the client or someone associated with him or her is threatening, stalking, or assaultive toward the psychologist.

In general, termination should be viewed as a phase of the professional relationship; it is an essential aspect of each client's treatment. As such, it should first be discussed during the informed consent process. This is especially true for students and trainees who typically stay at a service delivery location for a limited and predetermined period of time. Clients should know how long the psychotherapist will be there and what procedures are in place for transferring their care to another professional should ongoing treatment be needed when the student psychotherapist leaves that site. Termination should be planned and, when possible, occur by mutual agreement. It should not come as a surprise to the client.

Abandonment implies that the client's treatment needs are not being adequately addressed. It may occur when termination is mishandled or even during the process of psychotherapy, for example, as a result of lack of psychotherapist availability between sessions or inadequate coverage arrangements during periods of absence for the psychologist. Making such arrangements and keeping clients informed are essential for preserving the psychotherapy relationship. Psychologists should make arrangements with colleagues in advance to ensure that clients are not abandoned should the psychologist become ill, disabled, or die. Those in private practice may wish to consider a professional will to meet this obligation.

Key Recommendations

✓ Consider termination planning as an essential component of each client's treatment plan.

✓ Discuss all potential limitations to treatment such as finances, insurance coverage, and one's availability from the outset as part of the informed consent process.

✓ Ensure that clients have your emergency contact information, know how to reach you between sessions, and know when extratherapeutic contacts are appropriate.

✓ During anticipated periods of unavailability, always ensure adequate coverage by a competent colleague, obtain clients' consent to share information about their treatment with this colleague, and provide clients with emergency contact information.

✓ Document all discussions of termination and all related agreements with clients and colleagues.

✓ When entering a new employment position, make clear arrangements for client care should you become unable to continue their treatment.

✓ Always attempt to work through termination issues and concerns with clients; avoid terminating services abruptly unless actions by the client or others necessitate rapid termination.

✓ Whenever possible, avoid termination with a client who is in crisis and avoid termination solely because a client has become unable to pay for services. Even if you decide not to provide the needed treatment, you must make a good faith effort to provide referrals and assist such clients with the referral process.

✓ Do not continue treatment when clients are not benefiting from treatment, when you are no longer competent to help them, or when your objectivity or judgment is impaired. When unsure about whether any of these circumstances exists, consult a colleague or ethics committee.

✓ Never terminate a client from treatment with the intention of initiating an inappropriate multiple relationship.

✓ Unless contraindicated, consider following up termination with a letter to the client reviewing the reasons for termination, any agreements and recommendations for continued services, the specifics of any referrals, and your offer to provide further assistance if needed. Keep a copy of this letter in the client's record.

See Standards 2.06, 3.12, 6.02, 6.04, 10.01, 10.09, and 10.10.

Responding to an Ethics Complaint, Licensure Board Complaint, or Malpractice Suit

Although most psychologists go though their entire careers without having an ethics complaint, licensure board complaint, or malpractice suit levied against them, how psychologists respond to such actions should they occur can have a significant impact on the outcome. Facing a complaint or malpractice suit can be an extremely stressful and anxiety-arousing experience. It can also be quite costly in terms of time away from work, expenses associated with a legal defense, and emotional turmoil. Although prevention is certainly the best approach, should a psychologist become the focus of a complaint or suit, knowing how best to respond is essential.

Contacting an attorney to seek legal advice is an important first step when psychologists are notified of a complaint or charge. They should not take matters into their own hands or try to resolve it themselves. It is best for psychologists not to contact the complainant to try to work things out or to share their thoughts on the complainant's actions. This may only make matters worse for them, and anything they say or do may be used against them during the hearing or trial. In the case of a malpractice suit, psychologists should contact their malpractice insurance carrier immediately. They should share all information relevant to the case and listen carefully to all advice given. They should be familiar with the details of their malpractice insurance policy. Some policies allow psychologists to select their own attorney, whereas others require psychologists to use an attorney assigned by their carrier. It is also strongly recommended that psychologists purchase coverage for disciplinary hearings, not just malpractice suits. These can be costly as well, and the additional coverage may eventually pay big dividends.

Psychologists should be sure their documentation is in order and that all relevant records and materials are pulled together. They should include all case notes, agreements, consultations, and any other materials related to the particular individual's treatment. Their attorney will want to review all the specifics of the case with them. Psychologists should remember that they will be judged by prevailing professional practice standards. They do not have to be perfect or achieve perfect results in their work with clients. But, they do have to demonstrate how they have met the standards of care of the profession. As such, psychologists should be familiar and be able to reference relevant sections of the American Psychological Association Ethics Code, relevant state laws and regulations, and relevant practice guidelines that apply to their case.

Psychologists should not attempt to provide ongoing treatment if a current client files a suit or complaint against them. Instead, they should provide appropriate referrals and work to ensure a smooth transition to another provider if treatment needs still exist, remaining professional at all times. Psychologists' ability to remain objective and impartial will likely be impaired. They should be sure to practice ongoing self-care and seek support as they go through this trying experience. Even frivolous complaints can be very stressful and costly. If confidentiality concerns prevent psychologists from sharing details of the complaint with others, they should seek personal psychotherapy to assist them in navigating this challenging and demanding process.

Key Recommendations

✓ Never contact the complainant and try to informally resolve the matter.
✓ Never modify your documentation after the fact in an attempt to bolster your defense against charges.
✓ If an investigator shows up at your office requesting to interview you or obtain copies of records, politely decline until you have had a chance to confer with your attorney. Do this even if the investigator says it will be better for you if the two of you talk and work things out informally.

Unless a valid court order is presented, decline and state that your attorney will contact the investigator with a response.

✓ Never try to defend yourself alone in any ethics complaint, licensure board complaint, or malpractice suit. Seek the advice of a competent attorney and allow this individual to represent you in all hearings and other administrative or judicial proceedings. Have all communications with adjudication bodies or opposing counsel go through your attorney.

✓ Understand the procedures used by the investigating agency or judicial authority. Work with your attorney to best represent you in this forum.

✓ Know the standard of care for the services you provide and in the setting in which you practice.

✓ Be able to demonstrate the appropriateness of the actions you took and the treatment you provided. Be able to articulate the rationale behind all decisions made.

✓ Be prepared to demonstrate your competence in providing treatment to the particular individual on the basis of his or her history and presenting problems. Have your curriculum vitae up-to-date and gather all transcripts, certificates, licenses, and other relevant credentials to demonstrate your training and experience.

✓ Strive to minimize the stress of this situation on your ongoing work with other clients. Practice ongoing self-care; obtain personal psychotherapy, supervision, or consultation; and use ongoing self-reflection to help determine whether you should limit or restrict your work activities.

Key Ethics Resources for Psychologists

Ethics Guidelines and Resources

American Psychological Association (APA) Ethics Office: http://www.apa.org/ethics/

- Ethical Principles of Psychologists and Code of Conduct (APA Ethics Code)
- APA Ethics Committee Rules and Procedures
- Statement by the Ethics Committee on Services by Telephone, Teleconferencing, and Internet
- Guidelines for Ethical Conduct in the Care and Use of Animals (APA Board of Scientific Affairs)
- Research With Animals in Psychology (APA Board of Scientific Affairs)
- Columns by the Director of APA's Ethics Office, Stephen Behnke, Ethics Rounds
- HIPPA for Psychologists: http://www.apapractice.org/apo/hipaa.html# (APA Practice Organization)

APA Practice Guidelines: http://www.apa.org/practice/prof.html

- Determination and Documentation of the Need for Practice Guidelines
- Guidelines for Psychological Practice With Older Adults
- Record Keeping Guidelines

- Guidelines for Child Custody Evaluations in Divorce Proceedings
- Guidelines for Psychological Evaluations in Child Protection Matters
- Guidelines for Psychotherapy With Lesbian, Gay, & Bisexual Clients
- Guidelines on Multicultural Education, Training, Research, Practice, and Organizational Change for Psychologists
- Criteria for Evaluating Treatment Guidelines
- Criteria for Practice Guideline Development and Evaluation

American Psychological Association Insurance Trust (APAIT): http://www.apait.org/apait/

- Risk Management Strategies and Sample Informed Consent Documents: http://www.apait.org/apait/resources/articles/

An Online Ethical-Decision-Making Resource

- Markkula Center for Applied Ethics: Decision Making: http://www.scu.edu/ethics/practicing/decision/framework .html

Web Site of Ken Pope: http://www.kspope.com

- Dual Relationships, Multiple Relationships, & Boundary Decisions: http://www.kspope.com/dual/index.php
- Ethics Codes & Practice Guidelines for Assessment, Therapy, Counseling, & Forensic Practice: http://www.kspope.com/ ethcodes/index.php
- Ethics & Malpractice: http://www.kspope.com/ethics/ index.php
- Fallacies & Pitfalls in Psychology: http://www.kspope.com/ fallacies/index.php
- Informed Consent in Psychotherapy & Counseling: http:// kspope.com/consent/index.php
- Psychology Laws & Licensing Boards in Canada & the United States: http://kspope.com/licensing/index.php
- Sexual Issues in Psychology Training & Practice: http:// kspope.com/sexiss/index.php
- The Therapist as a Person: http://kspope.com/therapistas/ index.php (includes therapist's guide to making a professional will)

Selected Books on Ethics

Bersoff, D. (2008). *Ethical conflicts in psychology* (4th ed.). Washington, DC: American Psychological Association.

Keith-Spiegel, P., Whitley, B. E., Balogh, D. W., Perkins, D. V., & Wittig, A. F. (2002). *The ethics of teaching: A casebook* (2nd ed.). Mahwah, NJ: Erlbaum.

Knapp, S. J., & VandeCreek, L. D. (2006). *Practical ethics for psychologists: A positive approach.* Washington, DC: American Psychological Association.

Koocher, G. P., & Keith-Spiegel, P. C. (1998). *Ethics in psychology: Professional standards and cases* (2nd ed.). New York: Oxford University Press.

Nagy, T. (2005). *Ethics in plain English* (2nd ed.). Washington, DC: American Psychological Association.

Pope, K. S., Sonne, J. L., & Greene, B. (2006). *What therapists don't talk about and why: Understanding taboos that hurt us and our clients.* Washington, DC: American Psychological Association.

Pope, K. S., & Vasquez, M. J. T. (2007). *Ethics in psychotherapy and counseling: A practical guide* (3rd ed.). San Francisco: Jossey-Bass.

Key Psychology Organizations

- American Psychological Association: http://www.apa.org/
- APA College of Professional Psychology: http://www.apa.org/college/homepage.html
- APA Practice Organization: http://www.apapractice.org/
- American Psychological Association of Graduate Students (APAGS): http://www.apa.org/apags/
- American Board of Professional Psychology (ABPP): http://www.abpp.org/
- Canadian Psychological Association: http://www.cpa.ca/
- Canadian Register of Health Service Providers in Psychology: http://www.crhspp.ca/
- Council of Provincial Associations of Psychology: http://www.crhspp.ca/cpap/
- European Federation of Psychologists' Associations: http://www.efpa.be/
- National Register of Health Service Providers in Psychology: http://www.nationalregister.org/
- State and Provincial Psychological Associations: http://www.apa.org/practice/refer.html

Licensing Boards

- Association of State and Provincial Psychology Boards: http://www.asppb.org
- Licensure Board Contact Information: http://www.asppb.org/about/boardContactStatic.aspx
- Psychology Licensing Board Disciplinary Actions: http://www.apadiv31.org/LicensingBoardDiscipline.ppt
- What You Should Know About Licensing Board Disciplinary Procedures: http://www.apait.org/apait/download.aspx?item=Disciplinary_Complaint

Resources for Psychologists in Distress

✓ Advancing Colleague Assistance in Professional Psychology: http://www.apa.org/practice/acca_monograph.html

Continuing Education

Each of the following offers APA-approved home study continuing education (CE) in ethics and ethical practice:

✓ APA Online Academy: http://www.apa.org/ce/
✓ Association for Advanced Training in the Behavioral Sciences (AATBS): https://www.aatbs.com/
✓ At Health.Com: http://www.athealthce.com/
✓ CE4less.com: http://www.ce4less.com/index.aspx
✓ CE Seminars on Legal and Ethical Risk and Risk Management: http://www.apait.org/apait/resources/risk-management/seminars/
✓ ContinuingEdCourses.Net: http://www.continuingedcourses.net/
✓ National Association for Continuing Education: http://www.naceonline.com
✓ Professional Resource Press: http://www.prpress.com/ce.html
✓ Psy Broadcasting Corporation (PsyBC): http://www.psybc.com/
✓ Zur Institute: http://www.drzur.com/

CE requirements for each jurisdiction (including ethics CE requirements): http://www.ce4less.com/APAAccreditation.aspx

Index

Accountability
    delegation of work and, 53
    obligations, 16
Advertising
    descriptions of psychology education and training programs, 94–95,
        114–115
    false or deceptive statements in, 91–93
    in-person solicitation, 98–99
    statements by others, 93–94
    testimonials, 97–98
Americans With Disabilities Act, 58
Animal studies, 134–136
APA Code of Ethics. *See* Ethical Principles of Psychologists and Code of
        Conduct (APA Ethics Code)
Assessment
    competence for, 154–155
    explanation of findings, 158–159
    general obligations of psychologists, 145–148
    informed consent in, 149–150
    interpretation of results, 153–154
    release of test data, 151–152
    scoring and interpretation services, 156–158
    security of test materials, 159–160
    suicide risk, 189–190
    test construction, 152–153
    use of obsolete or outdated tests, 155–156
Authorship credits, 139–141
Avoidance of harm, 13–14, 61–62

Barter, 108–110
Beneficence and nonmaleficence, 13–14
Burnout, 53, 54

Children
    informed consent issues, 73, 74, 83
    mandatory reporting requirements, 193
Civil disobedience, 28
Clinical practice
    basis for scientific and professional judgments, 49–50
    with couples or families, 163–165
    delegation of work in, 50–53
    fees and financial arrangements, 106–110
    group therapy, 165–166
    informed consent issues, 71–74
    informed consent to therapy, 161–163
    interruption of services, 75–77, 172–173
    in managed care settings, 181–184
    organizational relationships, 74–75
    practitioner's personal problems affecting, 53–55
    professional collaboration, 70–71
    recording of therapy sessions, 82–83
    student therapy during training, 118–120
    termination of therapy, 173–174, 197–199
    therapy with those served by others, 166–167
    withholding records for nonpayment, 104–106
    See also Assessment; Documentation; Therapeutic relationship
Collection agencies, 107, 108
Collegial relationships
    consultations, 87–88
    fidelity principle in, 15, 16
    filing of improper complaints, 36–37
    informal resolution of perceived ethics violation, 30
    request to treat those served by others, 166–167
    sharing research data for verification, 141–143
Competence, professional
    for assessment, 146, 148
    basis for scientific and professional judgments, 49–50
    boundaries, 41–46
    delegation of work and, 50–53
    emergency services, 46–47
    false or deceptive claims regarding, 91–92
    maintaining, 48–49
    personal problems affecting, 53–55
    for test design, 152–153
Complaint investigation, 4
    cooperation with, 34–36
    due process considerations, 37–39
    improper complaints, 36–37
    response to complaint or accusation, 201–203
Confidentiality
    assessment data, 151–152
    common dilemmas, 80, 81–82, 83, 86, 87, 89
    consultations and, 8, 87
    disclosures, 85–86
    documentation obligations and, 83–85, 102, 103–104
    in ethics investigation, 36

informal resolution of perceived ethics violation and, 30, 31
limits of, 80–82
mandatory reporting requirements, 193–195
multiple relationships and, 65
obligations, 79
prepublication review and, 143–144
principles of ethics code, 21
professional use of confidential information, 88–90
recording research activities, 126–127
recording therapy sessions and, 82–83
reporting of perceived ethics violation and, 32, 33
safeguards against student disclosures in academic settings, 117–118
sharing research data for verification, 141–142, 143
third party requests for services and, 67, 68
Conflict of interest, 65–67
considerations in couples and family therapy, 164
Consultations
confidentiality and, 87–88
general guidelines for psychologists, 185–187
Continuing professional development
knowledge of diverse populations, 22, 41, 42, 45
professional competence, 41–46, 47, 48–49
Continuity of service, 75–77
Couples therapy, 163–165
Court-ordered services, informed consent issues, 72, 149
Credentials and licenses, claims regarding, 91–93
Culturally sensitive practice, 21, 22, 43, 45, 60–61, 148

Debriefing for research participants, 133–134
Deception
in advertising, 91–94
general obligations of psychologists, 17–18
reporting of research results, 136–138
reports to payors and funding sources, 110–111
in research, 17–18, 131–134
Delegation of work, 50–53
assessment, 154–155
Department of Agriculture Animal Welfare Guidelines, 136
Dignity and worth of individuals, 21–22
Discrimination
against clients, 57–58
harassment or demeaning behaviors, 60–61
maintaining respect for dignity and worth of individuals, 21–22
against participants in ethics investigation, 37–39
self-examination for bias, 58
Documentation
confidentiality considerations, 83–85, 102, 103–104
informed consent, 72
planning for interruption of services, 76, 77
recording of therapy sessions, 82–83
reports to payors and funding sources, 110–111
response to ethics or malpractice complaint, 202
scope of obligations, 101–102
withholding records for nonpayment, 104–106

Education and training
    accuracy of course description and contents, 114–117
    for assessment, 154–155
    evaluation of student performance, 120–121
    general obligations of psychologists, 113–114
    informed consent to therapy from trainee, 161–162
    research with students, 127–129
    safeguards against student disclosures in, 117–118
    sexual relationships in, 121–122
    student contributions to research, 139–141
    student therapy in, 118–120
Emergency services, 46–47
    suicidal client, 189–192
    withholding clinical records for nonpayment, 104–106
Enforcement of APA Ethics Code, 2, 23
Equal treatment
    discriminatory behavior, therapist's, 57–58
    obligations of psychologists, 19–22
Ethical Principles of Psychologists and Code of Conduct (APA Ethics Code),
        ix
    conflicts with other obligations or regulations, 5, 7, 14, 27–29
    ethical decision making and, ix–x, 5, 6, 7, 10, 23, 175–180
    Ethical Standards section, 2, 3, 23–24
    General Principles, 2, 3, 11–12
    historical and conceptual evolution, 1–2
    Introduction, 2, 3
    language, 5, 7, 23
    legal status, 2, 5, 6–7
    obligation to comply, 4, 6
    Preamble, 2, 3, 9–10
    purpose, 4–5, 9
    scope and comprehensiveness, 3–4, 6
    structure, 2, 3
    underlying values, 2
Exploitative relationships, 68–70

Family therapy, 163–165
Fees and financial arrangements
    barter, 108–110
    inducements for research participation, 130–131
    obligations for practitioners, 106–108
    referrals and, 111–112
    reports to payors and funding sources, 110–111
    withholding records for nonpayment, 104–106
Fidelity, 15–16
Forensic psychology, competence considerations, 42, 46

Gender identity, 21, 22
Group therapy, 165–166
Guidelines for Child Custody Evaluations in Divorce Proceedings, 45
Guidelines for Ethical Conduct in the Care and Use of Animals,
        45, 136
Guidelines for Practice With Older Adults, 45

Guidelines for Providers of Psychological Services to Ethnic, Linguistic, and
        Culturally Diverse Populations, 22, 45, 148
Guidelines for Psychotherapy With Lesbian, Gay, and Bisexual Clients, 22,
        45
Guidelines on Multicultural Education, Training, Research, Practice, and
        Organizational Change for Psychologists, 22, 45

Harassment or demeaning behavior, 59–61
Hippocratic oath, 62
Human rights
        basis of ethical decision making, 5, 7
        respect for dignity and worth of individuals, 21–22

Informed consent, 71–74
        in assessment, 149–150
        consultation relationships, 87, 88
        to couples and family therapy, 164
        for disclosure of information, 85, 89–90
        fees and financial arrangements, 106–108
        for group therapy, 165–166
        limits of confidentiality, 81
        mandatory reporting requirements and, 194
        multiple relationships and, 65
        nonpayment policy, 105
        obligations to report to payors and funding sources, 111
        organizational relationships, 74, 75
        for recording voices and images, 82–83, 126–127
        referral practices and compensation, 112
        in relationships with subordinates, 52
        in research, 124–127, 129–130
        termination of therapy issues, 197–198
        to therapy, 161–163
        third party requests for services and, 68
Insurance
        practice in managed care settings, 181–184
        reports to insurers, 110–111
        response to malpractice charge, 201–202
Integrity, 17–18
Interpretation for informed consent in assessment, 149, 150
Interruption of services, 75–77, 172–173

Justice, 19–20

Law
        applicability of APA Ethics Code, 2, 5, 6–7
        confidentiality, 79
        conflict with APA Ethics Code, 5, 7, 27–28
        response to ethics or malpractice complaint, 201–202
        unauthorized disclosure of clinical information, 85–86

Managed care settings, 181–184
Mandatory reporting requirements, 193–195

Media relations and use, 93–94
    broadcasting of professional advice or comment, 95–97
    See also Advertising
Misuse of work, 25–26
Multicultural practice, 22
Multiple relationship
    common challenges, 64
    conflict of interest, 65–67
    considerations in couples and family therapy, 164
    definition, 62–63
    delegation of work and, 50–51
    obligation to avoid, 63–64
    prevention, 64–65
    risk factors, 64

Organizational relationships, 74–75
    institutional approval of research proposals, 123–124
    managed care settings, 181–184
    third party requests for services, 67–68

Plagiarism, 138–139
Pro bono work, 15, 16
Professional relationships
    avoidance of harassment or demeaning behaviors in, 59–61
    avoidance of harm in, 61–62
    conflict of interest in, 65–67
    conflicts among obligations and regulations, 27–29
    cooperation, 70–71
    delegation of work and, 50–53
    discrimination against participants in ethics investigation,
        37–39
    exploitation in, 68–70
    fidelity principle in, 15–16
    justice principles in, 19–20
    multiple relationships, 62–65
    organizational relationships, 74–75
    third party requests for services, 67–68
    See also Collegial relationships; Therapeutic relationship
Public statements
    broadcasting of professional advice or comment, 95–97
    false and deceptive advertising, 91–93
    by others, 93–94
    promoting educational programs, 94–95
    testimonials, 97–98

Racial/ethnic bias, 21, 22
Reasonable behavior, 5, 7
Recording
    of therapy sessions, 82–83
    of voices and images in research, 126–127
Referrals
    fee arrangements, 111–112
    professional competency considerations, 41, 44, 47

    termination of therapy, 197
    unethical behavior, 43
Reporting of perceived ethics violation, 32–34
Research
    accuracy of public statements regarding, 91, 92, 93
    animal studies, 134–136
    avoidance of harm in, 61–62
    with clients, 127–129
    confidentiality in prepublication reviews, 143–144
    debriefing for participants, 133–134
    deception in, 17–18, 131–134
    delegation of work in, 50–51, 52
    inducements for participation, 130–131
    informed consent issues, 124–127, 129–130
    institutional approval, 123–124
    misuse of work or findings, 25–26
    plagiarism in, 138–139
    professional competence considerations, 41, 42
    publication credits, 139–141
    recording voices and images in, 126–127
    reporting of results, 136–138
    republishing of data, 141
    sharing data for verification, 141–143
    with students, 127–129
Respect for dignity and worth of individuals, 21–22
Resumes and professional experience claims, 91–93
Reviewing of material for publication, 143–144

Sanctions, 4, 6
Self-determination, right of, 21, 22
Sexual harassment, 59–60
Sexuality and sexual behavior
    avoidance of bias based on, 21, 22
    avoidance of harassment or demeaning behaviors based on, 59–61
    exploitative relationships, 68–70
    intimacies with former client, 171–172
    multiple relationships, 65
    relationship with client, 168–169
    relationship with client's relative or significant other, 169–170
    teacher–student relationship, 121–122
    therapy with former sexual partner, 170–171
Solicitation, 98–99
Special populations
    harassment or demeaning behavior toward, 60–61
    professional competence for work with, 22, 41–42
    therapist's discrimination against, 57–58
Standards for Educational and Psychological Testing, 147, 153
State regulation
    APA Ethics Code and, 2
    documentation and records maintenance, 102
    mandatory continuing education, 48
    mandatory reporting requirements, 193–195
    reporting of perceived ethics violation, 32

Suicidal behavior or ideation, 189–192
Supervision
    assessment, 154–155
    avoidance of harm in, 61–62
    delegation of work and, 50–53
    evaluation of supervisee performance, 120–121
    exploitative relationship in, 68–69
    general guidelines for psychologists, 185–187
    sexual relationships in, 121–122
Syllabus description, 116–117

Technology
    automated test administration and scoring, 156–158
    broadcasting of professional advice or comment, 95–97
    confidentiality and, 81, 82
    recording, 82–83
Termination of APA membership, 4
Termination of therapy, 173–174, 197–199
Testimonials from clients, 97–98
Therapeutic relationship
    avoidance of harassment or demeaning behaviors in, 59–61
    avoidance of harm in, 61–62
    client testimonials, 97–98
    exploitative relationship, 68–70
    fidelity in, 15–16
    multiple relationships, 62–65
    research with clients, 127–129
    respect for rights and dignity of individuals, 21–22
    sexual intimacy with client's relative or significant other, 169–170
    sexual intimacy with current client, 168–169
    sexual intimacy with former client, 171–172
    stresses for practitioner, 53, 54
    termination of therapy issues, 198
    therapy with former sexual partner, 170–171
    third party relationships and, 66–68
    unfair discrimination against client, 57–58
Third party relationships
    conflict of interest issues, 66–67
    requests for services, 67–68
Trust relationships, 15–16, 69

Violations of APA Ethics Code, 4
    discrimination against participants in ethics investigation, 37–39
    failure to comply with ethics investigation as, 34–35
    improper complaints, 36–37
    informal resolution, 30–32
    reporting, 32–34
    request for deferment of adjudication, 34, 35
    response to complaint or accusation, 201–203
    See also Complaint investigation; Sanctions
Vulnerable populations, 21
    mandatory reporting requirements, 193–195

Workshop and educational presentations, 94–95

About the Authors

Jeffrey E. Barnett, PsyD, is a licensed psychologist in independent practice in Arnold, Maryland, and a professor on the affiliate faculty in the Department of Psychology at Loyola College in Maryland. He is a diplomate of the American Board of Professional Psychology in Clinical Psychology and in Clinical Child and Adolescent Psychology and is a distinguished practitioner in psychology of the National Academies of Practice. Dr. Barnett is a fellow of seven divisions of the American Psychological Association (APA) and a member of the APA Ethics Committee. He previously served two terms on the Ethics Committee of the Maryland Psychological Association with one term as chair. He is an associate editor of the journal *Professional Psychology: Research and Practice* and editor of its Focus on Ethics section. Dr. Barnett has presented and published widely on issues relevant to ethical practice in psychology. He is active in leadership positions in the profession of psychology and has served as president of the Maryland Psychological Association and of several APA divisions.

W. Brad Johnson, PhD, is an associate professor of psychology in the Department of Leadership, Ethics, and Law at the United States Naval Academy and a faculty associate in the Graduate School of Business and Education at Johns Hopkins University. A clinical psychologist, he is a fellow of the APA and has served as a member of the APA Ethics Committee. Dr. Johnson has authored more than 80 articles and book chapters as well as 9 books in the areas of ethical behavior, mentor relationships, and counseling. Among his most recent books are *Write to the Top: How to Become a Prolific Academic* (2007), *On Being a Mentor: A Guide for Higher Education Faculty* (2006), and *The Elements of Mentoring* (2004). He is a contributing editor to several journals in the field of psychology and is past president of APA Division 19 (Society for Military Psychology).